THE FOUNDRY

The Foundry

(Re)Formed by the Triune God

CARTER MCCAIN

WIPF & STOCK · Eugene, Oregon

THE FOUNDRY
(Re)Formed by the Triune God

Copyright © 2025 Daniel Carter McCain. All rights reserved. Except for brief quotations in critical publications or reviews, no part of this book may be reproduced in any manner without prior written permission from the publisher. Write: Permissions, Wipf and Stock Publishers, 199 W. 8th Ave., Suite 3, Eugene, OR 97401.

Wipf & Stock
An Imprint of Wipf and Stock Publishers
199 W. 8th Ave., Suite 3
Eugene, OR 97401

www.wipfandstock.com

PAPERBACK ISBN: 979-8-3852-5349-4
HARDCOVER ISBN: 979-8-3852-5350-0
EBOOK ISBN: 979-8-3852-5351-7

VERSION NUMBER 09/04/25

New Revised Standard Version Bible, copyright 1989, Division of Christian Education of the National Council of the Churches of Christ in the United States of America. Used by permission. All rights reserved.

This book is dedicated to

William J. "Billy" Abraham, a mentor whose influence far outstripped the time spent together.

Contents

Acknowledgments | ix

Introduction | 1

CHAPTER ONE
What Is the World? | 13

CHAPTER TWO
Who Is the Son? | 22

CHAPTER THREE
Re-Formed by the Son (Incarnation) | 32

CHAPTER FOUR
What Is the Flesh? | 45

CHAPTER FIVE
Who Is the Spirit? | 55

CHAPTER SIX
Re-Formed by the Spirit (Indwelling) | 65

CHAPTER SEVEN
Who Is the Devil? | 77

CHAPTER EIGHT
Who Is the Father? | 85

CHAPTER NINE
Re-Formed by the Father (Imitation) | 93

Conclusion | 104

Bibliography | 111

Acknowledgments

THERE ARE SO MANY PEOPLE without whom this book would not exist, or would be much less readable. To my wife, Karen: thank you for believing in this book more than I did at times, for sacrificing time and money so I could have time to write, for your prayers and comments, and for your encouragement. Thank you as well to all those who contributed to this manuscript through prayer, comments, and suggestions: Larry Easton, Kreshelle Marquis, Denise Duke, Cynthia Hight, Jacque Walker, Adam Walker, Dan and Jen Bennett, Luis and Laura Hernandez, David Baldwin, and Kara Davis.

Introduction

THIS BOOK WAS BORN of three desires.

The first desire is for Christians to embrace the Trinity. By this I mean not merely assenting to the doctrine of the Trinity but to see more in the Father, Son, and Holy Spirit than a faith to be professed or a puzzle to be solved. We believe in a personal God, one with whom we seek intimacy and who seeks intimacy with us. This is the whole-being embrace of a lover, instead of the mere intellectual embrace of the philosopher. But in practice many of us fail to give and receive that intimacy, and even more of us fail to understand how God being triune does anything other than complicate the matter. A lack of understanding of the Trinity (how can something be both three and one at the same time?) means we struggle to enter into worship of the Trinity in anything more than name only. In this book I will try to describe the Trinity in terms that are easy to understand, show how the Trinity relates to other things Christians hold dear, and suggest some practical exercises by which we might become better acquainted with the Father, and with the Son, and with the Holy Spirit.

The second desire is to help people who may never formally study theology. You don't have to attend graduate school to gain at least a passing familiarity with some of the thinkers who have influenced, sometimes decisively, the direction of Christian thinking about God. And in building this familiarity, one is empowered to live and worship with expanded depth. Towards this end, I will be pulling from a variety of thinkers from the early church to the present, sometimes in quotations and sometimes in passing references. For some of you this will be more than enough. For others, you will want to go deeper. I include a bibliography of references, some of which directly shaped this book, others which have shaped me.

The third desire is for Christians to champion a view of salvation that expects real transformation in this life—and sees it happen. The consistent and recurring command of the Scriptures is to be holy, to live a life that looks more and more like the life of Jesus. Yet countless believers feel so trapped that they conclude either that such transformation is a myth or that they are uniquely broken. The psalmist declares, "I believe that I shall see the goodness of the Lord in the land of the living" (Ps 27:13).[1] However, a great many fail to see meaningful, lasting progress in becoming more like Jesus despite their best efforts. And for the life of them, they can't figure out why. This book will focus on describing in detail what God has done and is doing to make this transformation possible, and to provide guidance on how we cooperate with God in our continued growth into Christlikeness.

We all know the story. God made a perfectly good world and made perfectly good human beings to shepherd and cultivate it in his name. He made them in his image so they could create with him: naming and building and loving. However, when given the option to continue in a relationship of love and dependence on God or forge our own way, humanity chose to try to go it alone: to know things without God, to do things without God, to call our own shots. And as the effects of this tragic decision rippled throughout creation, everything got worse. We got trapped in death-dealing cycles of thinking, feeling, and acting. Alienated from God, each other, and even ourselves, we continued to hurt and be hurt, throwing all of creation into disarray and bondage.

Therefore, Jesus comes to do what only he can do. Being fully God, he brings to bear the infinite resources of divinity to rob sin, death, and evil of all the power they previously possessed. Being

---

1. Scripture references here and following are from the New Revised Standard Version (NRSV).

INTRODUCTION

fully human, he carves out a way of being in the world that makes it possible for other humans to receive the Spirit and be like him. It was not God who needed to be reconciled to humanity, but humanity to God. But God took action to save us *as one of us*. Humanity brought the desolation off the fall, and so it would be humanity, in the person of Christ, who would bring the remedy.

So what is salvation? No doubt you've heard lots of answers to this, and there are lots of good ones. But I'll give you my simple summary This is the center, the core from which everything else flows, including forgiveness, eternal life, victory over evil, and growth in holiness.

Salvation is union with Christ in such a way that we participate fully in the life of the triune God and fully in the life of God's people.

Emphasizing full participation in the life of God's people is especially important in cultures which routinely stress the individual's strength, autonomy, and importance. The Western culture of which I am a part is an example of such a culture. Finding a severed thumb on the street would disgust us, but for some reason finding sincere Christians cut off from community doesn't distress us. We have forgotten or never known how things are supposed to be, so we don't feel revulsion when the lived reality of many churches is impotent and cold. As many of us have never known the incredible power of a life-giving Christian community, we don't know to long for it.

We have gotten used to a life without deep connection to God or to each other. We live hand to mouth, grasping at the scraps of connection when they are available and making do with what we know is far too little. Sometimes we struggle to think deeply, and we doubt whether routine connection is even possible on this side of heaven. We know we were made in God's image; we would get that right on the test (if there ever was one). But that seems so long ago and so far away. How do we get back there? Can we get back there? Does it matter? And what does any of this have to do with a foundry?

A foundry is a building that melts down metal in order to reshape it into various forms. It is a place of machines, of oil, of fire. For those who know me, it's laughable that I'd write a book with this title. I've never been to a foundry, let alone operated one. I'm not handy in the least; I dissolved into a puddle of tears assembling tricycles for my sons when they were toddlers. But there's something here for me, for us.

Despite the fact we are made in the image of the triune God and are filled with the Holy Spirit, we now partly bear the image of another. We struggle to change because we don't understand *why* we are so far off the mark in the first place. "If I was created good, how can I be this bad? How can it be this hard to get better?" We think these thoughts because we underestimate how deeply we have been formed by three things:

The World

The Flesh

The Devil

We don't understand what these are or just how deeply they have infected and twisted our reality, and so we underestimate our need to be re-formed by the Father, Son, and Holy Spirit. Or if we do feel our great need, then we miss how to go about having that need met. Not understanding the problem, we fail to understand the solution.

God brings salvation from the threefold onslaught of sin. He saves us by extending the eternal reality of his triune nature into space and time *for us*. The Father sends the Son on a mission of love, a mission the Son freely and gladly accepts. The Son becomes human in the person of Jesus Christ by the power of the Spirit. The Son and Father send the Spirit on a mission of love, a mission the Spirit freely and gladly accepts. The Spirit fills those who have been united to Jesus by faith, establishing their unity with each other and with Christ. This unity is what ultimately draws us back

INTRODUCTION

to the love and fellowship of the Father, which is truly the love and fellowship of the entire triune God. This book will trace each of the movements back into the heart of God, providing what I call "Opportunities to Practice" at the end of each chapter, which are designed to reinforce some of the key points and help you experience the change they can bring about.

I want to add a word quickly on what this book is *not*. I will not be providing arguments intended to convince the reader that the Trinity is a biblical concept or that God is, in fact, triune. There are many great books on such subjects, some of which I will include in the bibliography, but I will move far too quickly to convince anyone not already convinced. Instead, I will be assuming the reader is already committed to the truth of the Trinity as broadly defined within the bounds of classic Christian orthodoxy. This is summarized well by the Athanasian creed, one of the major Christian confessions of faith: "we worship one God in Trinity, and Trinity in Unity; neither confounding the Persons, nor dividing the Essence."[2] The creed goes further than this, and as we go through the persons, I will be fleshing out more of the orthodox faith. I focus on painting a fuller picture of the Trinity by connecting it to other core Christian doctrines and to the lived experience of sanctification. Peter Toon (1939–2009) in *Our Triune God* provides a helpful, pithy summary of what we will be exploring in this book:

> There is a movement of grace (creation, revelation, salvation) from God toward the world—from the Father through the Son and in/by the Spirit; and there is a movement of grace (faith, love, obedience) from the world to God—to the Father through the Son and in/by the Holy Spirit.[3]

Part I of this book focuses on our formation by the world and the need for re-formation by the Son. Chapter 1 discusses the world as the systemic, structural manifestation of sin. It is the "way things work" that runs contrary to God: the institutions, the

---

2. This wording of the Athanasian Creed comes from Schaff, *Creeds of Christendom*.

3. Toon, *Our Triune God*, 37.

priorities, the culture. We discuss several exemplars of this way of operating and dig into the difficulty of seeing the world as anything but the natural, even desirable, course our lives should take. Chapter 2 discusses the unique identity of the Second Person of the Trinity as the Logos and Son of God, as the one who makes God known to creation and in whose image humanity is created. By uniting himself to humanity in Jesus of Nazareth, the Son of God scandalized the religious establishment of the day and provided the answer to the sin of Adam. By reflecting on who the Son was before ever becoming incarnate, we understand better who God is and how he empowers us to live. Chapter 3 focuses on the theological and practical implications of the incarnation, the self-offering of God as a remedy to evil and sin. Jesus lives perfectly as a human, giving us an example of how we are to live. As our head, he enables us to follow and imitate him, enlivening us with himself so we can live the way he lives. As part of his body, the church, we learn to live in a community that is practicing living these realities out, enabling us to resist the destructive current of the world. For many, the idea of relying on the church as essential to our growth brings out every defense mechanism we have, including ones we didn't know existed. We'll talk more about this later, but the church is the single most important institution in our world despite her imperfections.

Part II focuses on the formation of the flesh—our flesh—and the need for re-formation in and by the Spirit. Chapter 4 gives a thorough account of what the flesh is and how it arises. As the world is the external manifestation of sin, the flesh is the internal one. Thoughts, feelings, and habits that further our estrangement from God and each other characterize the flesh, requiring a remedy. Chapter 5 focuses on the person of the Holy Spirit, the one who serves as the bond of love between the Father and the Son. The work of the Spirit in both creation and redemption reveals who the Spirit is and what his mission entails. That mission culminates in the formation of an empowered church, a visible community intended to mirror the eternal life of love of the Trinity. Chapter 6 discusses the power available to us through the indwelling of the

INTRODUCTION

Holy Spirit. The Spirit fills us to provide a new way of operating, with the ultimate goal of being effortlessly holy the way Jesus was. But as creatures with the power of choice, we must cooperate with Jesus in our growth through practice. Though he will always lift the heavy end, we have to lift alongside him. We *get* to lift alongside him.

Part III focuses on our formation by the devil and the need for re-formation at the hands of the Father. Chapter 7 provides the theological underpinnings behind Satan and demonic forces. Though coming into existence as angels, their fall corrupted them and precipitated our fall. The nature of the devil and demons is best revealed by examining what they do: deceiving us and lending power to the most destructive impulses and desires within us. Chapter 8 dials in on the nature and character of the Father, the one from whom the Son and Spirit proceed. Despite being the source or spring of life of the Trinity, the Father is in no way superior to the Son and the Spirit. We will discuss the way in which the love we encounter in Jesus is the very love of the Father, and how we have failed to bask in his love the way we were created to. Chapter 9 is the culmination of the book, highlighting the way in which sin is ultimately overcome in our lives and our world. Satan, as the hideous strength behind the world and the flesh, has not stopped trying to shape and influence us as a counterfeit to the love of the Father. Learning to rely on the Father in our vulnerability by imitating the life of God and resisting the devil is what weans us from the shame and fear of the "accuser."

This book is designed to be read with a group, and each chapter will be accompanied by exercises to be practiced and discussed together with others. Don't feel as if you have to do all the exercises; choose some that seem to fit where the group is and where you all sense it is headed. But don't do them alone. As will become clearer throughout the book, there are places we cannot get unless we get there together. A professor of mine once said, "If you want to see God, don't look in the mirror. Look at a crowd." This is right, but it's incomplete. If you want to see God, look at a crowd meaningfully united despite fierce differences, a crowd that is on mission, that wants more than merely its own survival and comfort. Finding a small group like this will be difficult, and being vulnerable with them will be even more so. But the result will be worth it.

As part of writing this book, I read about what happens at a foundry and watched videos of the process. When you melt down scrap metal, impurities known as "slag" rise to the top and are removed. This is part of the purification and refinement process, and it can happen multiple times depending on the quality of the starting metal and the desired purity of the finished product.

We should expect our impurities to arise as we draw close to the threefold Fire. And we should not expect it will only happen once. Many of us have struggled to believe and feel and act more like Jesus because we have not been ready for (or known we needed) a grace that looks and feels like fire. As Tenth Avenue North describes so powerfully in their song "Healing Begins," grace is a power that forcefully confronts the sin within us.[4] This idea might jar us because we've become accustomed to a view of grace that is passive, that is welcoming and accommodating but not confrontational. We think sin might attack, but surely grace wouldn't do the attacking. Yet Matt 16:18 tells us that "the gates of Hades will not prevail against [the church]." It isn't darkness that's advancing, but the kingdom love of God. Darkness is on its heels, and it's on the way out. But there are still battles to fight. And we have to be willing to train our hands for war.

We are invited to trust the God who will shake everything that can be shaken (Heb 12) because he is the same God who would not break a bruised reed (Isa 42). It takes the right kind of fire at the right time to temper a sword, to harden the metal so it is useful. My prayer is that this book will kindle or rekindle in you the holy fire of the triune God and his people. I emphasize his people again because community—true community—will equally expose us. And while we cannot escape God, we more readily flee community and need to be encouraged to push in rather than retreat.

I want to conclude this introduction with a sonnet by John Donne (1571/2–1631) who was an English priest and poet. I invite

---

4. Tenth Avenue North, "Healing Begins."

INTRODUCTION

you to make it a prayer for transformation, and to recite it aloud either by yourself or with your group. We will come back to it later in the book.

"BATTER MY HEART, THREE-PERSON'D GOD"

> Batter my heart, three-person'd God, for you
> As yet but knock, breathe, shine, and seek to mend;
> That I may rise and stand, o'erthrow me, and bend
> Your force to break, blow, burn, and make me new.
> I, like an usurp'd town to another due,
> Labor to admit you, but oh, to no end;
> Reason, your viceroy in me, me should defend,
> But is captiv'd, and proves weak or untrue.
> Yet dearly I love you, and would be lov'd fain,
> But am betroth'd unto your enemy;
> Divorce me, untie or break that knot again,
> Take me to you, imprison me, for I,
> Except you enthrall me, never shall be free,
> Nor ever chaste, except you ravish me.[5]

---

5. Donne, "Batter My Heart," 264.

PART I

World to Son

Chapter One

What Is the World?

PAUL WRITES IN EPH 2:1–3, "You were dead through the trespasses and sins in which you once lived, following the course of this world, following the ruler of the power of the air, the spirit that is now at work among those who are disobedient. All of us once lived among them in the passions of our flesh, following the desires of flesh and senses, and we were by nature children of wrath, like everyone else." We see in this short passage the summary of what we have been delivered from: the world, the flesh, and the devil. James, in condemning "bitter envy and selfish ambition" (Jas 3:14), deploys a similar threefold structure, dismissing them as "earthly [world], unspiritual [flesh], devilish [devil]" (Jas 3:15).

We will consider the flesh and the devil later in this book, but let's focus first on the notion of the world (Greek: *kosmos*). This does not refer to physical creation at all, nor to creatures as such, even the ones opposed to him. Given God's clear and repeated commitment to creation, we should not expect to see any condemnation of creation itself. The God who commands, "Love your enemies and pray for those who persecute you" (Matt 5:44) would not then fail to show such love himself. Instead, what we see condemned is the fallen ordering of human society and the current principles that govern human affairs. "World" refers to the institutions, cultural habits, and structures in human society that promote a vision for humanity that does not align with that of the kingdom of God. The world is the set of anti-God systems that are operative around us, and sometimes in and through us. They are the currents that force us downstream, against which we have to struggle if we want to grow closer to God and to meaningful Christian community. And these currents do not simply force us away from God; they force us toward something as well, something darker and with schemes of its own. More on that in chapter 7.

Maybe all of that is a bit too abstract to be helpful. First John 2:16 provides yet another threefold description, summing up the world as "the desire of the flesh [Greek: *sarx*], the desire of the eyes [Greek: *opthalmos*], the pride in riches [Greek: *bios*]." Let's consider each of these in turn to better understand the driving principles behind the world.

The desire or lust of the flesh is the appeal the world makes to what are often referred to as our baser desires, to the things we want in an almost instinctual, animalistic way. The world will present to us a rich panoply of pleasures and will hawk them as the satisfaction for our deepest needs. If mere presentation doesn't work, then such pleasures will be forcefully pushed such that we can't escape their presentation. If the pleasures grow dull or begin being ignored, the world will develop darker and more novel expressions and will work to convince us they will bring pleasure (or at least relief). The desires of the flesh are rooted in very natural desires and needs but are exaggerated and twisted to unnatural extents. So natural hunger which aims to prolong life and health may become eating far too much or only eating the finest foods. A natural desire for rest might become sloth or idleness. These are what lusts are: caricatures of otherwise natural and good desires, taking things that are beneficial within certain bounds and un-bounding them. The world is a system designed specifically to generate lusts and claims to satisfy them, but it only partially satisfies in order to prepare the person for even more ravenous lusts. What starts as meeting a legitimate need morphs into something that steals and depletes rather than sustains and satisfies.

The desire or lust of the eyes refers to an inordinate desire for interesting things, for intellectual pursuits and levels of understanding, or even for simply novel trifles to keep our attention. The focus here is on a kind of endless curiosity that seeks out more and more things to gaze at and to know, not because such looking and knowing are beneficial, but for their own sake. This kind of curiosity contents itself in long hours of movies and shows that do not edify, of trivia on useless facts. These things are the antithesis to spiritual disciplines, like study and meditation, which encourage prolonged, focused attention on things that produce life. The lust of the eyes has darker manifestations as well, through the seeking of knowledge through illicit means like horoscopes and mediums. Such knowledge here aims not at satisfaction of curiosity but at control, at a mastery of situations and even people, often for personal gain.

The pride in riches refers to the fervent satisfaction one feels in being better than others, of living a kind of life that others will envy and want to emulate. The phrase "pride in riches" works since a lot of the manifestations of this require wealth: the best clothes, the best homes, kids at the best schools, the best entertainment. However, we miss the real force of the point by rendering it this way. First because almost no one thinks of themselves as wealthy even when they are demonstrably so. And second because I have known many people, myself included, drenched with the pride of life who have had very little in the way of wealth. This manifests differently of course: a feeling of moral superiority for making certain life choices, disdain for others who do not invest their time or money the way you do. The pride of life finds a way to appeal to each of us, regardless of socioeconomic status.

As an example, many years ago I was part of a group that would host a weekly dinner and Bible study for the homeless in our area. We were almost all in college, and some of the people who joined in this work remain friends today. We were incredibly focused on building relationships with our homeless sisters and brothers. We prided ourselves on knowing our regulars by name and recognizing people (and being recognized) when we walked around downtown. We did some very good work, but we'd be lying if we said there wasn't some pride in it.

I remember having a particular conversation with some friends where we bemoaned the fact that we could get older people to give money to support our homeless ministry but couldn't get them to donate their time by joining us at a dinner, seeing what we did, and working to build relationships. We concluded they weren't really committed to the welfare of homeless people the way we were. What struck me only a couple years ago, now that I am one of those "older people," is this: we gave what was abundant for us (time), and they gave what was abundant for them (money). Meanwhile, most of us didn't give what was scarce for us (money) but chose to criticize them for not giving what was scarce to them (time). It is this comparison of yourself with others for the sake of concluding others as "less than" that best characterizes the pride of life. If you have a tendency to contrast yourself with others, you are to that extent susceptible to the pride of life.

Each of these lusts ultimately brings desolation to humans, some more quickly than others. There are, sadly, numerous examples of these kinds of desolation at work in our world. Marketing campaigns aim to make people feel inadequate or deficient if they don't look a certain way or own some particular trinket. Governments will find tens or hundreds of billions to wage war but argue there is no money to feed and clothe those who lack basic necessities. Corporations will encourage countless individuals to work long hours to the detriment of their health and relationships. Colleges and universities will speak publicly of commitment to truth and open inquiry but privately will discourage and silence dissenting opinions without just cause. Courts and public services demonstrably treat people of different skin colors differently. These are all examples of the world, of ways of operating to which God stands opposed.

Ever to hear someone flippantly say, "That's just the way the world works," when explaining someone pushing someone else down, using violence, or distorting the truth to get ahead? That's the world. That quiet, gnawing complacency we have because things seem to benefit us? That's the world. That sense of hopelessness that any other way of operating is bound to make us look silly, or worse? That's the world.

Some of these things are like the air we breathe, so common that we struggle to see them until they are pointed out, and we struggle to accept them as wrong even after they are. The world promises a number of things that in and of themselves are good: safety, security, meaningful work, a sense of purpose, even the ability to help others in some capacity. But its ability to deliver on such promises is negligible, its way of instructing us in achieving these things is suspect, and the amount of value they are given becomes death-dealing.

The real rub of it is that pursuit of otherwise good things for their own sake and to the detriment of seeking God is self-defeating. It's a fool's errand. Haggai 1 records the story:

> "Thus says the Lord of hosts: These people say the time has not yet come to rebuild the Lord's house." Then the word of the Lord came by the prophet Haggai, saying: "Is it a time for you yourselves to live in your paneled houses, while this house lies in ruins? Now therefore thus says the Lord of hosts: Consider how you have fared. You have sown much, and harvested little; you eat, but you never have enough; you drink, but you never have your fill; you clothe yourselves, but no one is warm; and you that earn wages earn wages to put them into a bag with holes.
>
> "Thus says the Lord of hosts: Consider how you have fared. Go up to the hills and bring wood and build the house, so that I may take pleasure in it and be honored, says the Lord. You have looked for much, and, lo, it came to little; and when you brought it home, I blew it away. Why? says the Lord of hosts. Because my house lies in ruins, while all of you hurry off to your own houses. Therefore the heavens above you have withheld the dew, and the earth has withheld its produce. And I have called for a drought on the land and the hills, on the grain, the new wine, the oil, on what the soil produces,

on human beings and animals, and on all their labors."
(Hag 1:2–11)

There is a deep sense that what the temple meant to Haggai is now found in the personal and communal lives of believers (1 Cor 3:16). One way, then, to understand the critique the Lord offers of us in the voice of Haggai is to critically examine our tendencies to deprioritize intimate seeking of God in solitude and in community for the sake of other things. There are a great many people who are diligent at work, diligent with the care of their families, and diligent in a wide variety of personal pursuits, yet never achieve the goals for which they work so hard. There may be many reasons why this is so, but in some cases it is because God knows that to reward diligent work in the world not accompanied by diligent work on the soul would be ruinous.

When Jesus commands us to seek the kingdom of God and righteousness first and foremost (Matt 6), he means to redirect our first focus away from diligent work in the world. His command isn't a blanket promise that faithfulness produces material wealth. There are a great many people, both now and throughout history, who have been deeply faithful and yet poor, hungry, and thirsty. It is instead a direct denial of the lie of the world that one needs to seek one's own welfare and security first and God second (if at all). It is this lie that leaves people bankrupt, sometimes financially but always spiritually. Because the truth of it is this: you can't seek God second. To not seek God first is to miss him entirely. God cannot be encountered in that way. Or perhaps it is better put this way: any god you can seek in your spare time once you've gotten the "real work" out of the way is a false god. It is an idol, an empty myth.

There's a reason why Paul warns in 1 Tim 6:10, "For the love of money is a root of all kinds of evil, and in their eagerness to be rich some have wandered away from the faith and pierced themselves with many pains." There's a reason why the Bible talks more about the ethics of making, saving, spending, and giving money than it does about sex or murder or any number of other "moral" subjects. Money, more than any of the rest, is shorthand for safety, security, protection, and stability. To love those things, to seek them on their own terms, is to push out of our minds and hearts space for the love of God. And it does not take very much money to do so. Any amount we have plans for how to spend will suffice.

James identifies several other ways of operating that are rooted in love of the world rather than the love of God: "conflicts and disputes" (Jas 4:1) to get our own way, spending what we get primarily on our own pleasures. The message of the world is, "Want more and more, get more and more, take care of yourself more and more. Spending time doing much of anything else is a waste unless it serves you in some way." Agreement with the world kills any kind of genuine generosity as giving becomes a tactic rather than a joy. Agreement with the world kills any kind of legitimate peace or harmony within yourself or with others. We begin to think, "Anyone who doesn't think like me or act like me is the enemy, unless they can benefit me in some way."

The really insidious thing about the world, the thing that leaves people feeling powerless in the face of it, is the inability of any one person to do much of anything about it. These ways of operating are so entrenched that we can't escape them just by relocating ourselves. The desert fathers and mothers of the third and fourth centuries tried exactly this, fleeing the prosperous and wicked cities, forming small monastic communities or becoming hermits, and embracing lives of sometimes radical asceticism. Some of the most powerful writings of the Christian tradition came out of the flight from civilization, but these fathers and mothers communicated that the battle within themselves was greater in these settings; they fled the world only to find they brought the world with them in the form of the flesh.

Efforts to reform the world likewise face tremendous opposition. Innumerable structures and institutions have either been built for the purpose of furthering these agendas or have their livelihood dependent on them: political parties and governments, companies and financial institutions, schools and educational methodologies, public services and justice systems, even churches and entire religious views. It isn't that these cannot change or be changed: the end of chattel slavery is one glorious example. But almost inevitably, the end of one ill gives rise to more. Social evil seems to evolve but not to die. And those committed to improvement of society will be dismissed by many as naïve optimists, especially by those drinking deeply from polluted streams.

Finally, the power that feeds the world is not merely human or social but infernal. Thus, Paul writes, "For our struggle is not against enemies of blood and flesh, but against the rulers, against the authorities, against the cosmic powers of this present darkness, against the spiritual forces of evil in the heavenly places" (Eph 6:12). "Cosmic powers" here has the same root in Greek as world, and so what we find as the animating principle behind worldly powers are spiritual forces. Paul isn't saying that there aren't real battles against people. These forces find manifestation in flesh and blood, in humans and groups of humans. Humanity is complicit and even a catalyst in the furthering of evil in our world, but it is not the source.

We will be discussing throughout this book the remedies to these ills and the tools with which these structures can be dismantled. These will ultimately be found in a supernatural community that will impress upon us a certain way of life and demand of us intimate and growing participation. The irony is worth noting here. The world will promise a great many things but end up impoverishing us. The alternative to the world will demand a great many things but end up making us whole. The challenge will be found in who to believe and to follow.

WHAT IS THE WORLD?

OPPORTUNITIES TO PRACTICE

1. To discover the effect social media has on how you think and spend your time, go for a day (or a week!) without it. No Facebook, Instagram, Twitter/X, Youtube, etc. Note how easy or difficult this is for you and what you tend to do to fill the time that was previously spent on these sites. Prayerfully reflect on why you are drawn to social media and why you have a hard time limiting the amount of time you spend on it. Discuss your experience with the group, and talk about whether you expect to take similar fasts in the future or not, and why.

2. Think of a way you behave that is in opposition to the life of Jesus but that you cannot seem to let go of despite your best efforts. Don't focus on some besetting sin that society in general thinks is wrong, like theft or drug addiction. Identify something that is expected or even rewarded by society but opposed to God's way of being in the world. This might be how you treat others, how you spend your time or money, or something else entirely. For example, God convicted me about the amount of time and energy I spent planning for retirement. He has shown me I tend to be fear based, relying solely on myself to provide instead of leaning on him. Talk through what makes it seem so inescapable and why you think people struggle to see it as wrong. Give an example or two of what you think living differently might look like.

3. Find an opportunity to serve someone who you dislike who can be of no benefit to you whatsoever, who is in no position to repay you. If you can, serve them without them having known you've done so. Bonus points if they are from a different religion, different political view, or both! As you serve them, note any tendency to pride, to self-satisfaction, or to judgmentalism. Confess these to your group without giving away the nature of the service you provided or to whom.

Chapter Two

Who Is the Son?

It was the one, true God who became incarnate as Jesus of Nazareth, but it was specifically the Second Person of the Trinity who did so. This one is called the *Logos* in Greek, the Word of God, though the usual definition of logos as "word" does not do justice to its philosophical depth. The word "geology," for instance, refers to the study of the principles and rules (-logy) about the earth (geo-). The "-logy" has the same root as logos, helping us understand more of the underlying meaning. The sense here is that the Logos is the divine thought, the perfect expression of God's mind and intent. The Logos is the agent of creation, the Word of God spoken in Gen 1, and so it is supremely fitting that the Logos would be the one to become incarnate, to take full possession of created reality and to pull it into the very life of the Trinity. Since we were created through him, it is right that we will be re-created through him. That is precisely what salvation is: re-creation in, through, and by Christ.

The one who is called "Logos" is also called "Son." The Father calls Jesus "Son" at his baptism (Matt 3:17, Mark 1:11, Luke 3:22, John 1:34) and transfiguration (Matt 17:5, Mark 9:7, Luke 9:35), Jesus refers to himself as the Son numerous times (e.g., Matt 12:8, Luke 19:10), and even the apostle Peter professes this fact (Matt 16:16). However, Jesus bears the title "Son" in two different ways. The first is in reference to the eternal begetting in the Trinity, meaning being God before creation even existed. The other is in reference to the temporal begetting in the body of the virgin Mary. Begetting isn't a word we use very often. The Greek term is *gennao* and means to produce a descendant or offspring.[1] Begetting is simply making a thing of the same kind as yourself. So I might create a painting, but I can only beget a human child. Cats beget cats. Humans beget humans. God begets God. And this is the core of the unique teaching about God found in Christianity: there is both distinction (Father and Son, Logos and Origin) and unity (a single God) in the divine.

Another critical New Testament account of the identity of the Son is provided by Paul in Col 1:15–20. The language and structure of these verses have led many scholars to label it as the "Christ hymn," one that may very well have predated the writing of Colossians and may not have been written by Paul. There is frequent repetition of phrases and themes, two sections (creation and redemption) that closely parallel each other, and Greek phrases that "set it off" from what comes before and after. Let's look at the text:

> He is the image of the invisible God, the firstborn of all creation; for in him all things in heaven and on earth were created, things visible and invisible, whether thrones or dominions or rulers or powers—all things have been created through him and for him. He himself is before all things, and in him all things hold together. He is the head of the body, the church; he is the beginning, the firstborn from the dead, so that he might come to have first place in everything. For in him all the fullness of God was pleased to dwell, and through him God was pleased to reconcile to himself all things, whether on earth or in heaven, by making peace through the blood of his cross. (Col 1:15–20)

Whew. There is so much there worth reflecting on. The language hearkens us back to Genesis and the creation account, stressing the frequent Pauline connection between Christ and Adam. In

---

1. Danker et al., "γεννάω," *Greek-English Lexicon*, 170.

Paul's thought, which would later find a home in writings such as *Against Heresies* by Saint Irenaeus (130–202) and in those of countless other thinkers, Jesus is the "new Adam." He is the one who came to undo the sin of Adam that has plagued the human race and provided humanity a new start (for Saint Irenaeus, a "new Head"). The Christ hymn also reveals Christ as the center of both creation and redemption, a place occupied only by God in Jewish thought. Paul then piles phrase upon phrase to describe the eternal identity of Jesus of Nazareth.

With regard to creation, Jesus is

- The image (Greek: *eikon*) of the invisible God: The Greek here is the word from which we get "icon," a pictorial or artistic representation of something else. Christ is the visible, true revelation of God. He is the only way one can gain a knowledge of God as he is the visible self-revelation of the invisible God. He is also the model/template for humankind;

- The firstborn of all creation: Christ is the Messiah, the Supreme King of creation. "Firstborn" here is metaphorical just as in, for example, Ps 89:27 which says, "I will make him the firstborn, the highest of the kings of the earth." It is not literal, which would imply that Christ was a created being and created physically before any other human;

- The one by, through, and for whom all things were created: Everything that exists, including the hierarchy of angels, exists because of and for the sake of Christ. He is the beginning and end of creation, and it is only in him that it coheres and continues to exist.

- The head of the church: Christ is a "corporate person," one who contains all who are "in him." He is the sole unifying, governing, and sustaining force for and in the church. It gets its name and life from him, and him alone.

With regard to new creation (redemption), Jesus is

- The beginning, the firstborn from the dead: This phrase stresses both the temporal priority of Christ's resurrection (it was the first) and the fact that it is his resurrection that makes all others possible. His resurrection inaugurates (is the start of) the re-creation of all things;

- The one in whom the fullness of the Godhead dwells: Christ is the fulfillment of the Jewish temple, the physical location in which God chose to dwell and meet the nation of Israel. Christ's humanity is now that physical point of interaction. It is in him we encounter the true and full God. In him and him alone does God fully dwell/live/inhabit;

- The one through whom all things are reconciled: Christ is the agent of the restoration of relationship between Creator and creation, between himself as Lord and creation as subject. The end to which this restoration is aimed is cosmic peace (Hebrew: *shalom*), everything ordered properly and harmoniously.

In Colossians, Paul unpacks the same reality gestured to in John 8:58 when Jesus says, "Very truly, I tell you, before Abraham was, I am," using of himself the Greek equivalent (*ego eimi*) to the name that was reserved for God alone (YHWH). This wasn't just shocking to Jesus's contemporaries, it was an affront, the height of blasphemy. Here is a man claiming to be God. The response to this was predictable: "So they picked up stones to throw at him" (John 8:59). And had Jesus's claim not been true, his stoning would have been justified by the Torah. But because of the truth of this appalling statement, the response was a tragic revelation: "He came to what was his own, and his own people did not accept him" (John 1:11).

The incarnation of the eternal Son of God in the person of Jesus of Nazareth established a unique and unalterable relation between divinity and humanity, indeed between divinity and all creation. The human nature of the Son, while distinct from the divine nature, is not "other" from God in the way the rest of creation is. Jesus's humanity is not merely a creation of God, though it is that. It is, from the moment it comes into existence, God's own. It belongs as surely and completely to God as our bodies belong to us. "Belonging" isn't even the right word here. We do not merely possess our bodies; they are an essential part of who we are. Similarly, in the incarnation, humanity becomes an essential part of who Jesus is. The *hypostasis* (Greek for "person"[2]) of the Son is, therefore, the primary locus of union between God and creation, between infinity and finitude.

The Son of God becomes the Son of humanity in the incarnation. The real genius of the Council of Chalcedon (an ecumenical gathering of Christian leaders in 451 to determine the best expression of theological truths) was to affirm the consubstantiality (sameness) of Jesus with both God and humans. Jesus is divine in the same sense that the Father is divine, and human in the same sense that we are human. Chalcedon affirms this by relying on four terms: "unconfusedly," "unchangeably," "indivisibly," and "inseparably." Notice how each of these words contains a negative prefix. What these words make clear is what is *not* the case about Jesus's humanity and divinity:

4. Jesus isn't some kind of demigod like Hercules, 50 percent human and 50 percent divine. He is completely human and completely divine.
5. Jesus's divinity doesn't override his humanity. He remains like us in body and soul, albeit without sin.
6. Jesus's humanity doesn't detract from his divinity. He has never ceased being a member of the Trinity, the one in whom we live and move and have our being.
7. Jesus will never cease being human. Even now that he has ascended to the right hand of the Father, he retains his human mind, will, and body.

Though such statements about what is *not* the case (theologians call them apophatic statements) are helpful, we rightly want more. What does it mean for Jesus to be both human and divine, and why does that matter for us?

---

2. Danker et al., "ὑπόστασις," *Greek-English Lexicon*, 925.

Quite often our own humanity is taken as the paradigm case to which we must make Jesus fit; he must be human in the sense we perceive ourselves to be human. This approach is compelling for a few reasons: it clarifies that Jesus must have a true body, a true human soul, a true human will, and so on. This sameness is important because of a key principle about our salvation: "For we do not have a high priest who is unable to sympathize with our weaknesses, but we have one who in every respect has been tested as we are, yet without sin" (Heb 4:15). However, using our humanity as the model won't work for one, simple reason: our humanity is marred by sin. Though we remain truly human, we are human in a deficient, obscured manner. Christ's humanity was perfect from the moment of conception due to the hypostatic union. "Hypostatic union" is the theological term for the union of humanity and divinity in the person of Christ. In Christ we see what humanity was created to be. His humanity teaches us about our humanity, not vice versa.

The incarnation makes our own restoration to perfect humanity possible and shows us what the fullness of a human life looks like. It is in this sense that Christ can be called "Son of God" according to his humanity, because he lives a life of unbroken, intimate fellowship with and obedience to God. He is the Son of God according to his divinity by nature, but he is the Son of God according to his humanity by the power of the Spirit. The Spirit overshadows Mary in his conception (Luke 1:35) and descends upon him in baptism (Mark 1:10), with the result that Jesus is full of the Holy Spirit.

The fact that there are two senses in which we can call Jesus "Son of God" does not mean that there are two sons. We cannot attribute certain acts of Christ merely to his humanity or divinity; we must attribute both to a single subject. Rightly understood, the incarnation means we can say "God suffered" and "man restored life to Lazarus" without impugning the divine nature or falsely elevating human nature. What Christ does, all of Christ does. Thus, we ought to see the miracles Christ performed as both a sign of his divinity and of the possibilities present for humanity when indwelled by the Spirit. It is because of the latter that the apostles (and we ourselves) carry the true authority and power of God, derived from Christ and brought about by the agency of the Spirit. Jesus's relationship to the Spirit per his humanity is one of need (it is the Spirit who equips and anoints him for ministry) and following (it is the Spirit who leads him into the wilderness and who sends him on mission). In this he serves as both a forerunner and example for the rest of us. "Very truly, I tell you, the one who believes in me will also do the works that I do and, in fact, will do greater works than these" (John 14:12).

Because of the detail the Scriptures provide on the life and ministry of Jesus, and because of his unique role as Mediator between God and humanity (1 Tim 2:5), most have an easier time approaching him in thought and prayer than the Father or the Spirit. Yet the entire Godhead—Father, Son, and Spirit—invites us into fellowship with them through Jesus. George Herbert (1593–1633), a seventeenth-century English poet, captures this invitation and our response well in his poem "Love (III)."

> Love bade me welcome: yet my soul drew back,
>   Guilty of dust and sin.
> But quick-eyed Love, observing me grow slack
>   From my first entrance in,
> Drew nearer to me, sweetly questioning
>   If I lacked anything.
>
> "A guest," I answered, "worthy to be here":
>   Love said, "You shall be he."
> "I, the unkind, ungrateful? Ah, my dear,
>   I cannot look on thee."
> Love took my hand, and smiling did reply,
>   "Who made the eyes but I?"
>
> "Truth, Lord; but I have marred them; let my shame
>   Go where it doth deserve."
> "And know you not," says Love, "who bore the blame?"
>   "My dear, then I will serve."
> "You must sit down," says Love, "and taste my meat."

So I did sit and eat.[3]

Herbert captures well an experience I and countless others have had: grasping the enormity of what "Love" offers in the way of connection, and immediately feeling guilt and shame. We know—or think we know—that we don't belong. We don't dare voice it at first, so we "grow slack," but Love pursues us with sweet questions, the goal of which is to ensure we have everything we need. We fess up that we aren't worthy to be there, and Love emphasizes that one day we will be, that our destiny is to be made worthy. We, deeply familiar with ourselves and our ugly bits, dare not even look upon Love. Love emphasizes the goodness of our creation and the fact that we were made for this connection. We begin to beat ourselves up over how much we've messed up ourselves and our lives. Love redirects us to the cross as the place on which all of that has been dealt with.

And so, having our shame answered at every turn but still knowing we feel it and wanting to wallow in it, we offer one final bargain. We'll stay around, but only if we are allowed to exhaust ourselves in service. This has the illusion of holiness; service is, after all, part of the right response to the love of God. However, service motivated by guilt and shame does not unite us more closely to God, it does not bear any fruit worthy of repentance (Matt 3:8). It is simply another way of trying to reinforce our unworthiness instead of rejecting it. And so Love refuses our self-righteous attempts to work our way into belonging, instead offering the only command of the poem: "You must sit down . . . and taste my meat."

This command communicates an important truth: the remedy to guilt and shame is found not in service but in allowing ourselves to be served and fed. Peter had to face his embarrassment and false humility on the eve of the institution of the Eucharist when Jesus said, "Unless I wash you, you have no share with me" (John 13:8). True humility isn't refusing to be served by Jesus but the recognition that the depth and profundity of our lack is such that reception of everything Jesus has to offer is the only

---

3. Herbert, "Love (III)."

remedy. When Love intones sweetly, "You shall be he," it is not a denial of what is lacking but a refutation of the belief that lack is disqualifying.

And what is the meat of which the poem speaks? It is nothing less than the life of the Incarnate God:

> So Jesus said to them, "Very truly, I tell you, unless you eat the flesh of the Son of Man and drink his blood, you have no life in you. Those who eat my flesh and drink my blood have eternal life, and I will raise them up on the last day; for my flesh is true food and my blood is true drink. Those who eat my flesh and drink my blood abide in me, and I in them. Just as the living Father sent me, and I live because of the Father, so whoever eats me will live because of me." (John 6:53–57)

It is by feasting on Christ, by receiving from him by faith everything he offers us, that guilt and shame will be abolished and we will be made the kind of people who belong. And if the language of eating the flesh and blood of Jesus reminds us of the Eucharist, it should not come as a surprise. Communion is one of the most crucial places in which Christ feeds us with himself, serving us in order to knit us more closely with him and with one another. There are multiple other ways in which we feast on Christ: studying the Scriptures, prayer, fasting, service, and much more. We will discuss most of these in this book. Yet from the formation of the church, the Eucharist has held a special place.

OPPORTUNITIES TO PRACTICE

1. Choose one of the Gospels (Mark and John are both good options) and read it aloud as a group, everyone taking turns. Read the entire Gospel in one sitting. What strikes you differently than when you read it silently and privately? Which parts stand out to you? How does reading it all at once help your understanding?

2. One of the earliest practices of the church was to spend extended time reflecting silently and prayerfully on crucial moments in the life of Jesus: his temptation in the wilderness, his wrestling in the garden of Gethsemane, his words cried out from the cross, etc. Choose one of these as a group and begin in prayer asking God to help you encounter God and yourself in new ways through this reflection. Then spend time (thirty minutes or more) in silent reflection. During this time, feel free to jot down notes, draw pictures, or otherwise engage physically in the reflection. Then discuss as a group.

3. Next time your church offers the Eucharist or Holy Communion, go as a group (or as smaller groups if that is more feasible). If your church does not routinely offer Communion, find a faithful local church that does that you can attend and receive from. In advance and during the service/liturgy, think prayerfully through what it means for Jesus to feed us with his body and blood. What is on offer? What is the benefit for us?

Chapter Three

Re-Formed by the Son (Incarnation)

So why did the Son become human, and what is the significance of the cross? This question deserves a book all its own, and hundreds have been written on it. However, I want to highlight one aspect: the overcoming of sin for humanity.

> There is therefore now no condemnation for those who are in Christ Jesus. For the law of the Spirit of life in Christ Jesus has set you free from the law of sin and of death. For God has done what the law, weakened by the flesh, could not do: by sending his own Son in the likeness of sinful flesh, and to deal with sin, *he condemned sin in the flesh*, so that the just requirement of the law might be fulfilled in us, who walk not according to the flesh but according to the Spirit. (Rom 8:1–4; emphasis mine)

Since the contagion of sin has been passed along via the shared brokenness of our humanity, the incarnation connects the power of divinity with the great need of humanity. By forming and claiming the humanity of Jesus as his own, God brings his immeasurable power to bear directly on the human condition. And as sin

RE-FORMED BY THE SON (INCARNATION)

must be dealt with for humanity to be freed, God pours out his wrath and condemnation via the cross.

Now when we hear the word "wrath," we think we know what that means. We've experienced the wrath of others and our own wrath: the out of control emotions, the yelling, the overwhelming anger looking for someone or something to blame. But the Father is not out of control, and our own experience of wrath gives us a deep misunderstanding of the Father's wrath. His wrath is oriented to our good, not to some petty desire for a pound of flesh.

It is true that the Father's wrath is looking to hold something to account, but it is not Jesus who is the object of God's wrath. How could a loving and just Father condemn an innocent man, let alone his beloved Son? No, it is *sin* that comes under the fire of God's wrath. And since sin became rooted and entwined with our humanity, God takes on the fullness of our humanity to ensure his purifying wrath reaches everywhere sin has corrupted. "Where sin increased, grace abounded all the more" (Rom 5:20). God's wrath, far from being something that must be appeased in order for God to love us, is actually the manifestation—the revealing—of God's love against everything that has polluted and restrained us.

Related to this is a common misunderstanding. What is happening in Matt 27:46 when Jesus cries out from the cross, "My God, my God, why have you forsaken me?" Some have mistakenly taught that in this moment the Father and the Son were separated from one another, that the Father quite literally abandons the Son as the sin of the entire world—past, present, and future—comes to rest on him. They teach this because of two well-intentioned but mistaken interpretations:

1. They do not understand that Jesus is quoting from Ps 22, in which the psalmist provides an extended, prophetic prayer. He talks about the very real and present dangers of mistreatment and death but also discusses his selection by God from the womb and his future of proclaiming the goodness of God in a way that will bring future generations to the Lord. The psalmist is allowed to suffer, just as Jesus was allowed

to suffer and die, but there is no sense of any kind of cosmic god-forsakenness.

2. They combine Hab 1:13 ("Your eyes are too pure to behold evil, and you cannot look on wrongdoing") with 2 Cor 5:21 ("For our sake [God] made him to be sin") to conclude that the Father became unable to look upon Jesus, to see him at all, in this moment. However, the bulk of the Old and New Testaments involve the Father seeing sin, speaking to sinners, working on behalf of sinners. The point of Habakkuk isn't that the Father has to play peekaboo because of his holiness. If the Father is truly unable to look upon sin, he lacks the power necessary to see us and save us, which is blasphemy. The point of Habakkuk is that the intensity and perfection of the Father's holiness is such that it will ultimately tolerate no sin to remain. Habakkuk gives us the *reason* for the cross.

On top of the problematic understanding of Scripture, the idea that the eternal Father must forsake the eternal Son because of sin is deeply, theologically problematic—incoherent, actually. The Father, Son, and Spirit have been united from all eternity in relationships of love. They have never and will never exist apart from one another. To suppose that even the depths of human sin can for a moment sever that tie is to grant evil the power to change eternal realities, to change the triune God himself. Sin and evil have incredible, destructive power. But to God they pose no more threat than does a bug.

It is precisely the fact that the members of the Trinity can never be separated from one another that brings about a beautiful reality: Jesus is our entry point not only into his love for us but the love of the entire triune God. These are really one and the same. The love of the Father, the Son, and the Spirit is a single love, though we often experience this separately or sequentially. More than that, the incarnate Son of God is the *only* possible entry point into the love of the Trinity. One never encounters part of God because God does not have parts; to encounter a member of

RE-FORMED BY THE SON (INCARNATION)

the Trinity is to encounter the fullness of the Trinity. This doctrine is sometimes called *perichoresis*.

Puritan theologian John Owen (1616–1683) in *Communion with the Triune God* writes,

> Though there be no light for us but in the beams, yet we may by beams see the sun, which is the fountain of it. Though all our refreshment actually lie in the streams, yet by them we are led up unto the fountain. Jesus Christ, in respect of the love of the Father, is but the beam, the stream; wherein though actually all our light, our refreshment lies, yet by him we are led to the fountain, the sun of eternal love itself.[1]

Jesus is the beams and the streams. That is, he is the extension of the source of light and water which makes itself available to us. He is the one and only narrow gate, the only one in whom can be found eternal life. But beams come from the sun, streams from the fount, and the narrow gate leads one into a wide and fertile pasture. We miss the point of Jesus if we fail to accept his invitation to know and love his Father (John 14). And thus Owen continues,

> Would believers exercise themselves herein, they would find it a matter of no small spiritual improvement in their walking with God. This is that which is aimed at. Many dark and disturbing thoughts are apt to arise in this thing. Few can carry up their hearts and minds to this height by faith, as to rest their souls in the love of the Father; they live below it, in the troublesome region of hopes and fears, storms and clouds. All here is serene and quiet. But how to attain to this pitch, they know not.[2]

Here we encounter one of the flames of the foundry: contesting the lie that the Father is angry and unable to be pleased, or else that he is distant and aloof. Many seem to rest content with this view of the Father or else are not aware that relationship with the Father is something worth pursuing at all. This dissonance—basking in the love of the Son in a way that is isolated from Father

1. Owen, *Communion*, 112.
2. Owen, *Communion*, 112.

and Spirit—cuts us off from the true power of the incarnation and supports a false view of the Godhead. And cut off from this power, we fail to become the church as it is envisioned in the Scriptures.

The Bible structures its descriptions of the church using a variety of images: body of Christ, bride of Christ, people of God, and others. The intent is to show that the present people of God assembled by the Spirit and united to the Son live out and share in realities greater than those found outside of the church. Nevertheless, these present realities pale in comparison with what is to come. The visible church provides an image, however imperfect and partial, of heaven on earth and gets the privilege of partly manifesting heaven here and now. God's intent for the church, what it means to be the body of Christ, is to be the anti-world. The church is to be that place in which and through which currents flow to force us upstream and closer to God, counteracting and even negating the currents of the world. The church is to be that place to which we can run to see healthier models of thinking, feeling, and behaving. This is why believers simply will not thrive apart from purposeful, intentional involvement in Christian community. This is why churches cannot content themselves to be mere social clubs and cannot afford to tolerate or hide abuses and scandals.

For many of us, this is where we choose to get off the ride. We get our dependence on Jesus, but the idea of being dependent on other people is simply too much. We know how messed up we are and how many people we've hurt, and that makes it profoundly difficult to get close to others. "What if they find out what I'm really like?" we might think to ourselves. "And just look at them," we might also think. These people are messed up, and many of them are messing other people up. These people have hurt us, and some of them aren't even sorry for it. Whatever the church was *supposed* to be, many of us have concluded it is in reality something quite different.

There is much to say here, more than there is space to be said. However, I want to state very clearly that if you are at a church that is not just imperfect but toxic, or with leaders who have not simply made mistakes but are repeatedly wounding people without

RE-FORMED BY THE SON (INCARNATION)

repentance, leave and find a church and pastors who do not behave like that. There are a great many churches to which you can run that will treat you well and help you grow. Additionally, whatever our misgivings are about the church and its struggles, God has not laid out an alternative. There is no plan B. Each of us is called to learn from people who are imperfect, sometimes radically so. And we will suffer far more by cutting ourselves off from Christian community than we will by working through the hurts we receive and benefitting from the strengths of others. There will be parts of ourselves that will not be transformed if we do not find a way to live in close, personal relationship with others in community.

Yet, thank God, we will not have to tolerate this imperfect church forever. We still have much for which to long expectantly, as the rest of Rev 21 makes clear:

> I saw no temple in the city, for its temple is the Lord God the Almighty and the Lamb. And the city has no need of sun or moon to shine on it, for the glory of God is its light, and its lamp is the Lamb. The nations will walk by its light, and the kings of the earth will bring their glory into it. Its gates will never be shut by day—and there will be no night there. People will bring into it the glory and the honor of the nations. But nothing unclean will enter it, nor anyone who practices abomination or falsehood, but only those who are written in the Lamb's book of life. (Rev 21:22–27)

What awaits us is the perfection of everything we are as individual humans: body, soul, and spirit. What awaits us is the perfection of everything we are as corporate humanity: fulfilled relationships of mutual love and respect. Heaven is not simply for humans but for all of creation. God covenants with all of creation, and creation is groaning with labor pains (Rom 8:22) as it awaits its own consummation brought about through God's partnership with humanity. We cannot say what this will look like, but there will be not a single good we now see at work in creation that will not then be present more gloriously and more beautifully.

PART I | WORLD TO SON

The incarnation accomplishes not only a recovery of perfect humanity but an expansion as well. Human nature is deified in Christ: glowing at the transfiguration, conquering death in the resurrection, and being incorporated into the fullness of intra-Trinitarian life in the ascension. The humanity of Jesus is brought to the right hand of the Father, into the very presence of God. This is the first time ever humanity has experienced this depth of intimacy with God. Christ opens new possibilities for our entire race, realities unavailable even to prelapsarian (pre-fall) humanity. We are capable *here and now* of living a life that is both human and divine, even as we expect the fullness of that life to be revealed in the future:

> Beloved, we are God's children now; what we will be has not yet been revealed. What we do know is this: when he is revealed, we will be like him, for we will see him as he is. (1 John 3:2)

We seek to live lives of love and service because that is what humans were created to do and because that is the kind of life God lived for us in Christ. We are promised that the Logos who created everything will re-create everything and conform us to his image. Jesus Christ stands as both the source and *telos* (Greek for "purpose, intent, destiny"[3]) of all creation, as both Alpha/beginning and Omega/end.

Yet as we seek to lead such lives we will become aware of all the ways in which we fail to do so. We are not who we used to be, but we are also not yet who we will be. So what is the thing which both frees us from the past weight of our sins and prepares us to be made perfect? Forgiveness. But this forgiveness is often misunderstood.

I was leading a small class on Christian belief (I don't remember the exact subject matter that evening), and we were wrapping up with a question and answer session. A woman raised her hand and asked whether all of those who commit suicide are condemned to hell. The logic she had been taught was that suicide is a sin,

---

3. Danker et al., "τέλος," *Greek-English Lexicon*, 887.

RE-FORMED BY THE SON (INCARNATION)

and those who commit it do not have the opportunity to request forgiveness after. This question came out of nowhere for me, as we had not been discussing this subject. I told her that the forgiveness offered in the Son is not so limited or so legalistic. Imagine those who walked intimately with Jesus for years but struggled with some besetting sin (anger, lust, pride) that they were in a habit of resisting and confessing. If they gave into such a sin and happened to die before they could confess it, do we think they are forever cut off from grace? Of course not. Similarly, succumbing to depression and hopelessness in a moment does not negate a life lived in intimacy with God. But as I began to answer her question, she began to sob with relief. She had a dear friend who was a believer in Jesus but, in the depths of great pain, took their own life.

Forgiveness is a grace the Son makes available to us through his life, death, and resurrection. We tap into this gift through habits of faith, confession, repentance, and then extending forgiveness to others. The New Testament describes this in multiple places by contrasting "walking in sin/darkness" with "walking in the Spirit/light" (e.g., John 8:12, Eph 5:8). To receive forgiveness is not a case-by-case legal transaction in which we have to say or think the words each and every time. It is instead the loving posture of God toward those who have identified themselves with his Son and seek consistently but imperfectly to align their lives with him.

PART I | WORLD TO SON

OPPORTUNITIES TO PRACTICE

1. As we have seen, God is always on mission: always going, doing, and loving. Similarly, he calls his people to be a people on mission, a people sent. As a group, choose something to do together that will benefit people outside of your circle or church. Work at a soup kitchen, help someone move furniture who isn't able to do it themselves, visit a nursing home. In whatever you do, remind yourselves that your goal is to show the love of God.

2. Wounds we have suffered at the hands of fellow believers, or have ourselves afflicted on others, are some of the most difficult to process. Break into groups of two to three and share, privately and confidentially, some of the hurts or regrets you still carry that seem the most entrenched. Feel free to omit names and details as you see fit to maintain confidentiality. Once done, your partners should repent to you on behalf of the Christians who hurt you, or you repent to them on behalf of those you've hurt but might not be able to approach directly.

3. Spend an extended time alone or with others reflecting prayerfully on John 14:8–10: "Philip said to him, 'Lord, show us the Father, and we will be satisfied.' Jesus said to him, 'Have I been with you all this time, Philip, and you still do not know me? Whoever has seen me has seen the Father. How can you say, "Show us the Father"? Do you not believe that I am in the Father and the Father is in me? The words that I say to you I do not speak on my own; but the Father who dwells in me does his works.'" What does this mean the Father is like? What kind of God do we encounter in the person, words, and works of Jesus of Nazareth?

4. Often one of the hardest things for us to do is to forgive ourselves for the things we've done, especially if we have done them repeatedly over many years. Because we sometimes operate under the mistaken belief "If I was really sincere, I

RE-FORMED BY THE SON (INCARNATION)

would have beaten this a long time ago," we can carry great shame and anxiety over such sins. Make a list of things like this for you (everyone—or almost everyone—has them) and confess them to God. But this time, after you have done so, pray something like the following: "And I choose to forgive myself. God does not hold this sin against me, so I will not hold this sin against myself. God does not condemn me, so I will not condemn myself." Don't rush this; sit with it as long as you need to. The joy of forgiveness is not just the intellectual awareness of it, but the experience of a weight being removed.

PART II

Flesh to Spirit

Chapter Four

What Is the Flesh?

THE FLESH IS THE COLLECTION of thoughts, feelings, and behaviors that seek to meet legitimate needs in illegitimate ways. Satisfaction is pursued by our own power and for our own sake instead of in dependance on God and for his sake. The flesh originated in the fall of humanity in the garden of Eden. It is the broken humanity we have all inherited and that has twisted all interactions with ourselves, with others, and with God. Galatians gives an account of the manifestations of the flesh in human life: "fornication, impurity, licentiousness, idolatry, sorcery, enmities, strife, jealousy, anger, quarrels, dissensions, factions, envy, drunkenness, carousing, and things like these" (Gal 5:19–21). It would be worthwhile to conduct a detailed word study on these verses to better understand what each of these are and how they assault humanity. However, that study is beyond our scope here.

Many of you have no doubt heard the term "original sin." Original sin is sometimes taught and described as original guilt: Adam and Eve did a bad thing, and now we all are viewed as guilty. This view doesn't have any basis in Scripture and is a defective view of justice. Why should I be guilty of something someone else did? The more biblically rooted way of describing the current state of humanity, and one that finds expression in a variety of early church fathers, is not that we are guilty of Adam and Eve's sin but that their sin severed the relationship between humanity and God, twisting human nature and making it something less than what it was before.[1] Original sin is, therefore, the inheriting of a deficient nature, inheriting a lack. True human nature is what Adam and Eve possessed prior to the fall and what the Son took on in the incarnation. It is human nature as it was created to be: connected to God, oriented toward him, and receiving its sustenance from him. Having lost true human nature and possessing only a shell in its place, Adam and Eve passed it on, and we have continued to do the same. The flesh is what's left over once these ties to God are severed. What this means, perhaps shockingly, is that we are less than fully human. When we look at ourselves and others, what we are seeing is not full humanity.

Donne bemoans this weakened form of humanity in his sonnet we introduced back in the introduction: "Reason, your viceroy in me, me should defend, / But is captiv'd, and proves weak or untrue."[2] Reason, part of what makes us human, was created to fulfill a good purpose in us but has been twisted and weakened. It is incapable of performing its intended function due to impotence and corruption. However intelligent we are, we cannot count on always seeing the world rightly. We can echo these same sentiments for our bodies, prone to lack and disintegration. However diligent we are in care of our bodies, we cannot always count on them remaining healthy. We can echo them as well for our emotions, sometimes overpowering or misleading us. However sincere we are, we cannot count on desires always being beneficial to us. This is equally true of our wills, sometimes too passive and frail to choose the good even when we know it. However much effort we manage to put in, we cannot count on it being enough to achieve our goals.

If the flesh is *not* humanity as it was created to be, what is it? Put simply, the flesh is the manifestation of pride, of the desire to be

---

1. Some of the most important early developments of the doctrine of original sin were articulated by Saint Irenaeus of Lyons (130–202) and Saint Athanasius of Alexandria (296/8–373).

2. Donne, "Batter My Heart," 264, lines 7–8.

one's own god and determine one's own way of being in the world. The flesh is seeking one's own ends in one's own power. If this seems deeply similar to the account I gave of the world, it should come as no surprise. The world is pride enshrined in institutions, economies, cultural expressions, and interpersonal relationships. The flesh is pride enshrined in the human person, long practiced and habituated. The flesh forms the world, and the world reinforces and enables the flesh. And like the world, the flesh can be incredibly difficult to become aware of. Not on the face of things, of course: most of us are easily aware of all sorts of wrong desires and motivations we have. However, precious few realize the depths of it, partly because God in his grace shields us until we can bear it and partly because we are quite good at justifying our own desires and behavior. If you want a book that will haunt you in a "hound of heaven" kind of way, I highly suggest *I Told Me So: Self-Deception and the Christian Life* by Gregg A. Ten Elshof.[3]

I have experienced in my life both the grace of God saving me from shame by blinding me to my sins until the proper time and the pain of willful ignorance slowing my spiritual growth, sometimes with consequences to those I love. Of the two, the latter has occurred far more frequently. We are far more likely to flee to avoid self-realization of fault than we are to find God saying, "No further for now." As Jeremiah says, "The heart is devious above all else" (Jer 17:9). But that leaves us in a rough spot. How do we become aware of the things we aren't aware of and resist knowing?

As an undergraduate at the University of North Florida in Jacksonville, I had one of the most unique professors. He was an expert in philosophy, psychology, and religion, weaving them all into his lectures in sometimes surprising ways. One of the concepts he introduced us to was the Johari Window, a tool or exercise developed by Joseph Luft and Harrington Ingham in the mid-1900s. It is a way of gaining greater understanding of ourselves that looks like this:

---

3. Ten Elshof, *I Told Me So*.

PART II | FLESH TO SPIRIT

JOHARI WINDOW[4]

	Things we know about ourselves	Things we don't know about ourselves
Things others know about us	Public Self	Unseen Self
Things others don't know about us	Private Self	Hidden Self

Each of these "selves" make up who we are and who we believe ourselves to be.

- The Public Self is the set of things about us that we are aware of and most easily known by others. This includes things like the basics of our personality, our careers, the highlights of our upbringing, and the like.

- The Private Self is the set of things we know about ourselves but do not share with others and that are not easily known by others. This includes our inner thoughts and our secret actions.

- The Unseen Self is the set of things that others know about us that we are blind to. This includes both strengths and weaknesses that would surprise us, as well as tendencies we have of which we are unaware but are easily known by others. This is the self that tends to make people the most comfortable.

- The Hidden Self is the set of things that neither we nor others know about us, things that God alone knows.

Sometimes our sense of ourselves is accurate, sometimes not. But it is always incomplete. Though this rubric is secular in origin and incredibly simple, I was amazed at how the framework helped me understand myself better. I now had words to explain the times people were angered or hurt by me unintentionally, and the moments where someone knew something about me that surprised or even shamed me.

4. Luft and Ingham, "Johari Window." The version titled "Christian Response" was formulated by the author.

I also used this tool to begin seeking out greater self-awareness through the thoughts and opinions of others. This is always messy and a bit uncertain, both because people have their own blind spots that shape their opinions of others and because sometimes people are simply wrong. And when someone gets it right, it takes a level of maturity to acknowledge that fact and adjust our self-perception instead of retreating back into ignorance (denial), trying to explain or defend (justification), or shooting the messenger (anger). If these strike you as similar to the stages of grief, there's a reason: new self-knowledge, particularly of something embarrassing, easily causes grief.

How do we become aware of the things we need to know about ourselves, and what do we do with it when we find it? It took me years to realize that God has gifted the Christian tradition with a set of tools for just this purpose.

JOHARI WINDOW—CHRISTIAN RESPONSE

	Things we know about ourselves	Things we don't know about ourselves
Things others know about us	Confession (Public)	Community
Things others don't know about us	Confession (Private)	Contemplation

Throughout this book I'll be saying more about all of these themes and giving you opportunities to practice, but brief descriptions will suffice for now.

- Confession is the acknowledgement that something is wrong, agreeing with God against our sin. We can confess things directly to God, we can confess privately to one or two friends or mentors (Jas 5:16), and we can confess publicly or corporately as part of a small group or church. The Christian life demands all of these of us.

- Community is the group of people who know us well and by whom we are known. It is what the church ought to be, yet

PART II | FLESH TO SPIRIT

I believe precious few experience it. Many hunger for it but either don't know how to seek it out or are terrified of it for one reason or another.

- Contemplation is the deliberate, sometimes time-consuming, process of deeply and prayerfully considering God, the world, and ourselves. It is a means by which we become aware of our own thoughts, God's thoughts, and seek to replace the former with the latter.

Along the same vein of discovering more about ourselves and our motivations, we have lessons we can learn from regulated industries such as aerospace and nuclear power. I work for a biotech company and have led trainings on what is called "root cause analysis." This is a fancy term for a set of structured approaches to taking something that happened ("the problem") and figuring out why it happened ("the root cause") so that you can keep it from happening again. It's simple in most cases, but incredibly effective.

This helps explain why simply trying harder doesn't work. If I struggle with something like pornography and simply focus on the problem rather than the reason for it, I will put in *a lot* of effort with very little to show for it. This is how a great many Christians wage war against sin and the flesh: lots of trying, little growth. If instead we begin thinking and praying about why we struggle with certain things, it can be more beneficial.

In my personal and pastoral experience, people struggle with sins for vastly different reasons. Let me use sexual sin as an example: some struggle because they were abused either emotionally or physically, some because they are desperately lonely and need to feel connected, some because they carry tremendous anger and use pornography or sex as a way of dealing with that anger, some because they are emotionally numb and sex is the only thing that allows them to feel something. And the list can go on. For most, the reasons why we struggle are not readily apparent to us. We have to reflect, we have to pray, we have to hear the experience of others, and we have to get counseling. All of these are tools that allow us to get to our *why*.

As we probe deeper, we will typically find that our *why* is rooted in one or more aspects of the flesh, in the kind of frantic efforts to meet a real need in ways that are not in line with who we were created to be. And so, in the novel *The World, the Flesh, and Father Smith* by Bruce Marshall, Father Smith surmises that "the young man who rings the bell at the brothel is unconsciously looking for God."[5] This is no "pray the sin away" approach to spiritual growth. Not every sin goes away if we just read our Bible more, attend church more, worship more. All of those things no doubt benefit us, but they are a very small part of a very rich variety of options available to us. Fundamentally, Donne has it right: we need to be enthralled with God so we can let go of our obsession with ourselves. We need to be ravished by him so we no longer go begging for meager scraps from dusty tables. What we need are intentional practices we can engage in, repeatedly and intentionally, to bring us closer to the ravishing God.

Some of these practices will become apparent as we reflect on our *why*s and will require repeated practice because we won't be good at them at the start. For instance, if my struggles with sin are rooted in loneliness and feelings of isolation, I will need to seek to be known in community and to know others. However, if that was something that came naturally and easily to me, I probably wouldn't be in the spot I am. So it will take learning, practice, and help to overcome the things that have kept me from community.

There are also a known set of practices that have been proven over the centuries to draw us closer to God and to one another. Usually called the spiritual disciplines, they are things that we can put to practice that over time become habits that can sustain us through difficult or dry times. The classic treatment of spiritual disciplines by Richard Foster, in *Celebration of Discipline*, identifies twelve such practices: prayer, meditation, fasting, study, simplicity, submission, solitude, service, confession, guidance, celebration, and worship.[6] You will find that many of the "Opportunities to

---

5. Marshall, *Father Smith*, 108.
6. Foster, *Celebration of Discipline*.

PART II | FLESH TO SPIRIT

Practice" at the end of each chapter of this book are modeled on these practices, though they are pulled from other sources as well.

In the end, there isn't a single, all-encompassing list. We instead have to continually seek the ways in which the Spirit leads us to practice the overcoming of our flesh and the embracing of a different way of life. Over time, you will find ways of encountering the enthralling and ravishing God in precisely the places you struggle most to be enthralled and ravished. These methods will help you encounter not just God's love of humanity but God's love of *you*. Some may be unique because you are a unique person with a unique history, and God especially wishes to reach the parts of you that most resist being loved. Some practices you will stumble upon as you live out one of the historic practices and find it resonates more with you than it does with others. Some you will be led to by the Holy Spirit as you pursue the tried and true paths. As you become aware of such practices, lean into them.

WHAT IS THE FLESH?

OPPORTUNITIES TO PRACTICE

1. The primary practice identified in the Scriptures for taming the flesh and embracing humility is fasting.[7] Fasting is the intentional denial of something the body needs—typically food—for the sake of learning to rely on and encounter God more fully. Fast for a day, replacing the time normally spent on eating with something that draws you closer to God (reading Scripture, praying, worshiping, serving others, etc.). Then, when you break the fast, practice being thankful to God for both the fasting and for the food. Come back together as a group and share your experiences. If you cannot go a day without food without risk to your health, choose something else to fast instead.

2. Next time you say or do something embarrassing, don't do anything to explain or defend yourself—no reasons, no excuses, no apologies. If you can manage it genuinely (not in an exaggerated or deceptive way), even laugh at yourself. Learning to die to others' perceptions of you—to the false self that we show others and maintain at great cost—happens in small things rather than grand gestures.

3. Discuss as a group the following quote from Puritan Thomas Watson's (1620–1686) *The Doctrine of Repentance*: "Repentance does not take away a Christian's music, but raises it a note higher and makes it sweeter."[8] What is repentance? How does true repentance relate to joy and to a life lived well?

4. One of the most commonly used root cause analysis tools is called "Five Whys." Take some problem or sin you struggle with and write it down. Then reflect and pray through why you struggle with it, and write down what you learn. Then reflect and pray through why you struggle with that thing or what the source of it is and write that down. Do this up to five times or until you get to something fundamental. Then

---

7. For examples, see Ps 69:10, Joel 2:12, Ezra 8:21, and Isa 58.
8. Watson, *Doctrine of Repentance*, 103.

PART II | FLESH TO SPIRIT

engage in a discipline or practice that is intended to address that fundamental cause.

Chapter Five

Who Is the Spirit?

THE HOLY SPIRIT IS the Third Person of the Trinity, proceeding from both the Father and the Son.[1] Beyond that, many Christians struggle to articulate who the Spirit is or what he does. I want to begin this chapter by highlighting three fundamental truths on which the bulk of the Christian tradition agree and which help us rightly understand the person and work of the Holy Spirit.

The first is that the Spirit is truly and rightly described as both the Spirit of the Father (Matt 10:20, Eph 4:30, Rom 8:11) and as the Spirit of the Son (Acts 16:7, Rom 8:9, Gal 4:6). That is, the Spirit exists in deep, eternal connection with both Father and Son. If the Spirit were not the Spirit of the Father, he could not unite us to the Father. If the Spirit were not the Spirit of the Son, he could not unite us to the Son.

The second is that the Father's relationship to the Son is unique and different from the Father's relationship to the Spirit. I spoke in chapter 2 of the Father's begetting of the Son, of the generation of one who is completely equal to the Father. The procession of

---

1. I use here the Western formulation which includes the phrase *filioque* ("and the Son"), despite the fact that this clause was added to the Nicene Creed at a later date and is deeply contested by our Orthodox sisters and brothers. While I do not have space to go into the important, passionate, and sometimes tragic debates into this subject, the account of the Holy Spirit I give in this chapter is one upon which both East and West largely agree.

PART II | FLESH TO SPIRIT

the Spirit from the Father is commonly described as *spiration*, or a creative and life-giving breathing out. This is different from the begetting of the Son inasmuch as the Spirit is not a son or child of the Father but is still outside of time and gives rise to one who is completely equal to the Father and to the Son.

The third is that our surest and most reliable guide to what the Spirit is like is contained in the Scriptures. This is because the triune God is revealed most reliably and surely in the history of God's interactions with creation over time, culminating in the life of Christ. The reason so many get stuck in their attempts to understand the Trinity is that you can't understand the Trinity. The human mind is not capable of complete and total comprehension of an eternal reality. We can see and grasp only in part. And the best way to see and grasp God is by seeing what he does. So what do the Scriptures teach us about the Spirit's work?

The words translated as "Spirit" in both the Old Testament (Hebrew: *ruach*) and the New Testament (Greek: *pneuma*) have a deep, beautiful complexity. The words can mean "spirit," "wind," and "breath" and are connected to both order and life.[2] The *ruach Elohim* (Hebrew: "spirit (or wind) of God") hovered or swept over the waters at creation (Gen 1:2) just as the *pneuma hagion* (Greek: "Holy Spirit") came upon and overshadowed Mary in the incarnation (Luke 1:35). And similarly to how the Lord God formed humanity out of dust by breathing life into Adam's nostrils (Gen 2:7), we see Jesus breathing on his disciples and commanding them to receive the Holy Spirit (John 20:22). We see the Scriptures described as *inspired* by God in 2 Tim 3:16, which literally means "God-breathed." It is the Spirit's work in the writing, transmission, and reception of the Scriptures which enables them to uniquely bear the life and truth of God.

> What the Spirit has to provide he receives from the Son, as Jesus himself says, "I still have many things to say to you, but you cannot bear them now. When the Spirit of truth comes, he will guide you into all the truth; for

---

2. Danker et al., "πνεῦμα," *Greek-English Lexicon*, 738; Brown et al., *Hebrew and English Lexicon*, 924 (Strong's 7307).

he will not speak on his own, but will speak whatever he hears, and he will declare to you the things that are to come. He will glorify me, because he will take what is mine and declare it to you. All that the Father has is mine. For this reason I said that he will take what is mine and declare it to you" (John 16:12–15). This is a very important passage for two reasons. First, as Saint Athanasius (296/8–373) teaches us in book 1 of *Orations Against the Arians*, the role of the Spirit is not to sanctify Jesus so that he might become God.[3] Jesus does not stand in need of sanctification and does not need to become God because he is God by nature. Second, it reassures us that what the Spirit has to deliver to us he receives directly from the Son, who himself receives it from the Father. So what is ours is nothing less than the real and true heritage of the Father. So what is it that the Spirit delivers to us?

The Holy Spirit is described as the Spirit of truth. He was sent to guide us into all truth. This includes special revelation about who God is, what he's like, and what we must do. But as Billy Abraham (1947–2021) importantly notes in *Crossing the Threshold of Divine Revelation*, we are also radically dependent on the Spirit as the one who enables us to receive and understand that revelation. I'm going to quote him here and then discuss what he means, how it jives with the biblical witness, and what we do with it.

> Our cognitive capacities, habits, and dispositions need repairing, and they can be healed in part only by appropriate exercises and practices that enable us to switch perspectives and deal forthrightly with the light. This repair of our cognitive capacities is in turn made possible by the healing activity of the Holy Spirit, who searches and cleanses the soul of impurity and fear. Given the human alienation from God, given the ingenuity of human agents in finding ways to oppose the truth, there has to

---

3. Rusch, *Trinitarian Controversy*, 66 (from *Orations Against the Arians* 1.15).

be effective divine grace that will open the eyes of the soul and enable us to see the truth.[4]

Part of what has been broken by the cascading destruction of sin is our ability and willingness to think clearly. This is what we discussed via Donne's sonnet in the last chapter, and this is part of what Paul means in Rom 12 about the "renewing of our minds." We don't stand in need of being taught merely what to think, but how to think. We don't lack only the ability to see the truth, but the ability to be open to it and to sustain that openness over time.

In the incarnation, Jesus restored the possibility of right thinking by perfecting human nature, and in Christ we have that way of thinking available to us; Paul calls this "the mind of Christ" in 1 Cor 2. This way of thinking will take practice and will require sustained engagement of our wills, the humility to be corrected, and the openness to being sometimes painfully and avoidably wrong. It will also require the work of the Holy Spirit, who by indwelling us with himself makes it possible for us to have the mind of Christ. And we stand in need of this work not just at the moment of salvation (wherever one might choose to locate such a moment) but in every moment. It is only the Spirit that overcomes the flesh.

The Spirit works not only to renew our minds but to renew every facet of our lives so that we can look like Jesus and respond rightly to the will of the Father. The Spirit of Life restores the life we forfeited in the fall, setting us free from the law of sin and of death so that we are able to embrace God with our whole selves and operate out of this place of life. Because this Spirit of Life is the same one who raised Jesus from the dead, and because the Spirit now resides in us, we can be assured that we will one day share in a real, true, bodily resurrection just like Jesus (Rom 8). That is, everything that makes us human—body, mind, will, all of it—will drink of the life on offer by the Spirit and be gloriously transformed.

---

4. Abraham, *Crossing the Threshold*, 56.

And this isn't merely a restoration of what Adam and Eve possessed and rejected. Humanity isn't back to where it started but, through the glory of being united to divinity in the incarnation and the work of our Redeemer, is brought to a more beautiful state than Adam and Eve could have envisioned. This is called the *felix culpa* (Latin: "happy fault") because "where sin increased, grace abounded all the more" (Rom 5:20). Where Adam and Eve had a garden, restored humanity will have not only the garden but a new heavens and new earth (Rev 21:1). Where Adam and Eve had to deal with the serpent, all temptation and tempters will be banished. Where Adam and Eve could lose what they were given, restored humanity will have a kingdom without end (Rev 22:2–5).

I want to highlight that in Rom 8, it is only our bodily resurrection, the "revealing of the children of God" (Rom 8:19) that culminates in the delivery of all creation from its bondage, that is slated for the future. Everything else about our reception of the Spirit and what it is intended to accomplish in us is described by Paul in the present or past tenses. Everything else has been accomplished, and we are exhorted to a different manner of life: walking according to the Spirit, setting our minds on the Spirit, putting to death the deeds of the body. Yet there is something that knits together what has been accomplished with what will be accomplished, gesturing toward an even greater reality into which we've been sewn:

> For all who are led by the Spirit of God are children of God. For you did not receive a spirit of slavery to fall back into fear, but you received a spirit of adoption. When we cry, "Abba! Father!" it is that very Spirit bearing witness with our spirit that we are children of God, and if children, then heirs, heirs of God and joint heirs with Christ—if, in fact, we suffer with him so that we may also be glorified with him. (Rom 8:14–17)

We are given a spirit of adoption that assures us we are a true part of the family of God until the day in which we get to see the full sense of what that means. It is through the Spirit that we learn how to pray, to approach God as Father. As Saint Aquinas

(1224/6–1274) notes, the work of adopting sinners into the family of God is a Trinitarian work: the Father as the source or originator of the family, the Son as the example or pattern of sonship/daughtership, and the Holy Spirit who impresses upon us this pattern, who reshapes us into the image of the Son.[5] And what the Spirit is sent to do is not merely to refashion individuals into the image of Christ, but to form the family into which individuals are adopted. This community will mirror, in an imperfect, creaturely way, the eternal life of the Trinity. And the work needed to form such a group is no less supernatural than was the work to move individuals from death to life.

Though there is no single, definitive list of the gifts of the Spirit, 1 Cor 12 gives a representative sample: wisdom, knowledge, faith, healing, miracles, prophecy, discernment of spirits, tongues, and interpretation of tongues. Paul stresses that each of these is given for the "common good" and for the building up of a single body. That is, the culmination of the Spirit's work is not an empowered individual but a community of empowered individuals bound in love to each other and to the Father. The crowning work of the Holy Spirit is establishing the church, the body of Christ. Joined with Christ, its living head, the Spirit unites head and body together to form what Saint Augustine (354–430) described as the *totus Christus*, the whole Christ. The intent here isn't that Christ isn't complete without the church, but that the fulfillment of his messianic purpose is to establish and empower the community of faith as his body, as a means of grace to the world he loves.

So what is the role of the Spirit in the life of the church? Bertrand de Margerie (1923–2003), summarizing some of the elements of the thought of Saint Augustine, describes it as follows:

> The eternal Spirit of the Father and of the Son, their Communion and their reciprocal Gift, becomes then the Spirit of the Church in time, the temporal Gift which the Father and the Son make to her. The Breath of divine Love becomes the Soul of the universal Church, the Body of Christ. The principle of communion among Christians is

---

5. Aquinas, *Summa Theologica*, 3.23.2 ad 3.

at once consubstantial Communion between the Father and the Son and also between the Father and the sons in the Only Son.[6]

God's fundamental nature and character is Lover and Giver (1 John 4:8). Before the creation of time and space, God has existed as a unique community: one God, one divine consciousness "lived" out in a threefold way. Within God himself there is giving and receiving, loving and being loved. If this is difficult to understand, you aren't alone. There is nothing else like God; nothing in the world lives out this three-in-one reality in the same way God does. Nothing in finite creation can completely resemble infinite Creator. Yet if God is the one who created and formed us in his image, and if that image is triune, then perhaps there is something threefold about us. Saint Augustine thought so and discussed the mind and the life of rational beings like us as being comprised of memory, intellect, and will.[7] These three are different from one another, and yet the act of thinking inevitably involves the unity of the three. However, there is another image or example Saint Augustine provides, one that is more relevant to our point at hand.

Saint Augustine, Saint Aquinas, and countless others have described the person of the Holy Spirit as the "bond of love" between the Father and the Son.[8] The intent isn't to diminish the personhood of the Spirit but to emphasize his eternal role that we see reflected in salvation history. In book 8 of *The Trinity (De Trinitate)*, Saint Augustine uses the now famous analogy of Lover (Father), Beloved (Son), and Love (Holy Spirit) to help his readers understand the nature of God better.[9] In every act of human loving, there is one who loves, one who is loved, and the love itself, giving us a threefold image. So when we read "God is love" in 1 John 4, what we can understand is that God has been love from "before the foundation of the world" (John 17:24). God has been

---

6. De Margerie, *Christian Trinity in History*, 118.
7. Augustine, *Trinity*, 15.3.
8. Augustine, *Trinity*, 15.19.
9. Augustine, *Trinity*, 8.10.

love before even the angels were created because within God himself was the giving and receiving of love.

As it is the Holy Spirit who is the gift of God (Latin: *donum Dei*), the gift of love between the Father and the Son, so it is the Holy Spirit who sows the love of God into our hearts. The Holy Spirit is the gift of God to us as well, and through the indwelling of the Spirit (which we shall discuss later) we too get caught up into the relationship of love shared within the Godhead (Rom 5, John 17). As Jesus approaches his crucifixion, he begins speaking more plainly to his disciples about who he is and what he is going to do. It isn't accidental that this language of giving becomes more central. In the "high priestly prayer" captured in John 17, he focuses first on his own faithfulness to those the Father has given to him before transitioning to his own act of giving: "The glory that you have given me I have given them, so that they may be one, as we are one, I in them and you in me, that they may become completely one, so that the world may know that you have sent me and have loved them even as you have loved me" (John 17:22–23).

The gift of the Son to us is the glory of the Father, and the intent of that gift is to enable the community of the believers to be one, to be united in some way similar to and derivative of the union that exists between Father and Son. As Saint Athanasius puts it,

> The descent of the Spirit on him in the Jordan was a descent on us because of his bearing our body. Again, it happened not for the Word's improvement but for our sanctification, in order that we may share in his anointing, and about us it may be said, "Do you not know that you are a temple of God, and the Spirit of God dwells in you?" [1 Cor. 3:16].[10]

This is why division in the church is a scandal: it stands directly opposed to Jesus's own prayer to the Father and fails to uphold the unity the Spirit was sent to bring about. It is embracing fleshly ways of operating rooted in self-will instead of a spiritual harmony rooted in God's will. It is a failure to fully receive and make use

---

10. Rusch, *Trinitarian Controversy*, 89 (from Athanasius's *Orations Against the Arians* 1.15).

of the gift the Father gave the Son and the Son gave us. And what is that gift? It is the Spirit. What is the glory of the Father? Glory is something that reveals the nature and character of something. Glory is what makes something or someone known to us. And so to the extent to which we fail to be meaningfully united, we fail to make God known in the world. We grieve the Holy Spirit.

In the same way the Spirit works in individuals to restore proper thinking, so he works in the Christian community as a whole to lead us into all truth. Jesus's promise in John 16:13 has as its primary audience not the individual believer but the community of faith gathered across time and space, united in the common seeking and following of the one who has saved them. As Abraham notes, it would be "extremely odd for God to go to these lengths [to involve himself in human history through the incarnation] to make his name known and not provide critical assistance to the church as a whole in unpacking what this means."[11]

---

11. Abraham, *Crossing the Threshold*, 106.

PART II | FLESH TO SPIRIT

OPPORTUNITIES TO PRACTICE

1. As a group, set a timer for thirty minutes and put on soft, instrumental worship music. Sit in silence together, focusing your thoughts and prayers on one or two biblical examples of the Holy Spirit working: hovering over the waters of creation (Gen 1:1–2), coming upon Mary in the incarnation (Luke 1:34–35), descending upon Jesus like a dove in his baptism (Mark 1:9–11), lighting upon the disciples like tongues of fire at Pentecost (Acts 2:1–4). Ask the Spirit to help you understand what you are meditating on in a deeper way. When the timer goes off, share what you learned with the group.

2. The majority of Christians I have met have experienced one or more supernatural events: ways in which the goodness and grace of God have been made clear that aren't explainable in purely natural terms. This might look like a miraculous healing, knowledge of a person or situation that you couldn't have known on your own, or something else entirely. As a group, share some examples of things that have happened to someone in the group or that have been personally witnessed by someone in the group. Talk through what these teach us about God.

Chapter Six

Re-Formed by the Spirit (Indwelling)

SAINT SYMEON THE NEW THEOLOGIAN (949–1022) was a Byzantine writer and monk who died a millennium ago. He is called the "New Theologian" because the only other two canonized "theologians" of the Eastern church were Saint John the apostle and Saint Gregory Nazianzus (329–390), the latter of whom died five hundred and fifty years before Symeon and was one of the primary thinkers responsible for forming the doctrine of the Trinity. Illustrious company! Symeon gives us a critical account of the centrality of repentance in receiving the full life of God.

> I therefore entreat you, my fathers and brethren and children, let us endeavor to attain to purity of heart, which comes from paying heed to our ways and from constant confession of the secret thoughts of the soul. For if we, moved by a penitent heart, constantly and daily confess these, it produces in us repentance for what we have done and even thought. Repentance gives rise to the tear from the depths of the soul; the tear cleanses the heart and wipes away great sins. When these have been blotted out through tears the soul finds itself in the comfort of the Spirit of God and is watered by tears of sweetest compunction. By these it is spiritually fructified day by day so that it produces the fruits of the Spirit (Gal. 5:22f) and

PART II | FLESH TO SPIRIT

> in due time yields them like an abundant harvest of grain as an unfailing supply of food for the incorruptible and eternal life of the soul. When the soul by a good zeal has reached this state it is identified with God and becomes the house and the abode of the divine Trinity. It sees its own Maker and God clearly, and as it converses with him day by day it departs from the body and the world and from this air and ascends into the heaven of heavens. Borne aloft by the virtues and by the wings of God's love it rests from its labors altogether with all the righteous and is found in the infinite and divine Light, where the hosts of Christ's apostles, of the martyrs, of the blessed ones and all the powers on high sing in chorus together.[1]

There is a great deal to unpack in this quote, but I want to begin by stressing that the marvelous landscape Symeon paints at the end is absolutely *not* an image of our future resurrection and enjoyment of bliss in heaven. Symeon says this reality happens "day by day" and involves a departure from the body (in contemplation/prayer); the fullness of heaven will be something enjoyed by both body and soul. What Symeon is instead describing is the Christian life as it is meant to be experienced here and now. When Saint Paul in Eph 2:6 describes being seated with Christ in heavenly places, this is what he means. We are able to ascend to be with Christ: in this life, in our hearts, minds, and spirits; in the life to come, in our bodies as well.

The key to this ascent—and to enjoying the bliss of the Trinity in this life—is confession (agreement with God on the wrongness of some of our thoughts and actions) and compunction (grief over these wrongs and the ways in which they have twisted us and harmed others). Symeon uses this powerful image of the tears of such grief being the water for the fields of our souls. Without godly sorrow, there is no growth in virtue. Without being buried with Christ through baptism and repentance, there is no sharing in his life (Rom 6:4). Without the cross, there is no resurrection. Our lives must be cruciform (cross-shaped) if we wish to attain the glory promised to us.

1. Symeon the New Theologian, *Discourses*, 160 (from *Discourse 9* §10).

RE-FORMED BY THE SPIRIT (INDWELLING)

However, grief in and of itself produces no fruit. Sorrow can clear the landscape of our souls of clutter and mess, but it is only through the indwelling of the Spirit that we grow. The "comfort" of which Symeon (and the Scriptures he relies on) speaks is not merely the love of God blotting dry the tear-stained cheek. It is the love of God coming together (Latin: *con*) with us powerfully (Latin: *fortiter*) to transform us. It is for this reason the Spirit is described as the Comforter, the one who is sent to provide strength. Our sorrow does not produce or summon the Spirit of God, but it does yield our thoughts and wills to him. And thus yielded, we become saturated with his power.

But what exactly does the indwelling of the Spirit do to enable us to overcome sin? In chapter 3 of *The Mortification of Sin in Believers*, John Owen highlights three works of the Spirit necessary to overcome sin: (1) to cause the fruits of the Spirit to grow in us, which are virtues contrary to the vices of sin, (2) to consume the root of sin in us, weakening it to the point we can fight and be victorious, and (3) empowering us to participate in the death and sufferings of Christ. He describes the second point as

> a real physical efficiency on the root and habit of sin, for the weakening, destroying, and taking it away. Hence he is called a "Spirit of judgment and burning," Isa. iv. 4, really consuming and destroying our lusts. He takes away the stony heart by an almighty efficiency; for as he begins the work as to its kind, so he carries it on as to its degrees. He is the fire which burns up the very root of lust.[2]

In a foundry, chemicals are routinely added to the mix in order to give the metal the desired properties for its intended function. What we need is not simply to be purified, to have our slag removed. The vision and destiny God has for us doesn't just rely on getting sin out of the way. It depends on us having the divine life to draw from. By yourself, you will not have enough. You will not be enough. But you were never meant to do it by yourself. You were never meant to be left as you are. Spiritual poverty isn't

---

2. Owen, *Temptation*, 173.

disqualifying; it is a prerequisite! For those indwelled by the Spirit, what is lacking is not the power to overcome sin and bring Christ to bear in the world. To have received the Spirit is to have received the infinite God. What is often lacking is either the awareness of how to make use of this power moment by moment or the patience to continue fighting even in the midst of failures and struggles.

One of the things that keeps us from tapping into the power of the Spirit and the power of the community the Spirit is building is what I call the "Liturgy of the Bootstraps." Deep down, many of us believe the lie that we ought to be self-sufficient, that we ought to have it all together such that we can help others without almost ever needing help ourselves. We should be able to pick ourselves up by our own bootstraps and help others up at the same time! Almost no one will come right out and say this, but we engage in all sorts of verbal games that show this is the case:

- We ask for help in ways that are overly apologetic and reveal great shame.
- We offer help by minimizing what it costs us to do so, by pretending there is no sacrifice involved.

These games are what I mean by the Liturgy of the Bootstraps. We engage in these habits of conversation to safeguard our and others' sense of self-sufficiency. The trouble is that self-sufficiency is not a Christian view of the world; it is not who God designed us to be or the goal to which we should be striving. Extravagant generosity with boundaries is the way of kingdom life.[3] To counteract this tendency, we must intentionally engage in a different liturgy, a different way of speaking and acting. Fear of asking for help often comes from either pride or memories of how hard it has been in the past to ask for help and not receive it. Being humble to ask for help, and processing the negative emotions that come if that help is not provided by the community, is crucial for our growth. Generosity in the Christian sense flows out of a sense of lack and

3. For an excellent work on the importance of boundaries and how to maintain them, check out *Boundaries* by Dr. Henry Cloud and Dr. John Townsend.

need, not of power and self-sufficiency. We can only learn to be deeply generous to others by learning to acknowledge that we are deeply in need of others. Anything else runs the risk of promoting pride and self-righteousness.

As I reflect on the importance of weakness in the life of believers, I think back to Jacob's wrestling with God (Gen 32). The blessing itself was to go from being Jacob (one who follows or is behind) to Israel ("God contends"). By wrestling or contending with God, he became one for whom God contended, and became the father of a nation with the same name. But the cost of this was to come out of the encounter with a limp, one severe enough to have birthed a custom for the nation: "Therefore to this day the Israelites do not eat the thigh muscle that is on the hip socket, because he struck Jacob on the hip socket at the thigh muscle" (Gen 32:32). I wonder how many of us would contend long and hard enough with God for the sake of a blessing that we risked such an injury. And I wonder how much good would come if we did.

We are gradually learning to resist our unhealthy habits of thinking and acting, and to replace them with godly ones. This effort is empowered by the Spirit but inherently means practice and discipline on our part. The goal is to eventually be effortlessly holy, the way Jesus is. When I say effortless, I do not mean that there will be no suffering. A quick reading of Jesus in the garden of Gethsemane will dissuade someone of such a notion: he describes himself as sorrowful to the point of death, is sweating like drops of blood, and even pleads to be spared. "Yet, not my will but Yours be done" (Luke 22:42). What we do not see in Jesus here, what we in fact never see in the life of Jesus, is a moment of hesitation or debate on whether he would follow the will of the Father. He has a human will just like we have a human will. He desires to avoid suffering and death, just like we desire to avoid suffering and death. In Jesus, however, these natural, good desires are never tinged by sin and never pose the least obstacle to his resolution to obey the Father's will. As Maximus the Confessor (579–662), a seventh-century theologian, puts it, "He shows that all that matters is a perfect verification of the will of the Father . . . giving himself as a type and example of setting aside our own will by the perfect fulfilment of the divine."[4]

Imagine if someone insulted you and your family with the most hurtful things you've ever heard. Imagine they were rooted in enough truth that you couldn't immediately laugh them off or dismiss them, and so much lies and twisting of things that you could not conclude the person was simply mistaken. And now imagine that your immediate, strongest instinct was to forgive the person and bless them even in the midst of their tirade and even as you are hurt by their words. This is one example of what effortless holiness looks like. This gives us a picture of how Jesus operated.

"Yeah, but Jesus was God! Of course he could pull this off, but that doesn't mean I can." There's an element of truth behind this: Jesus was both man and God, possessing both a human will and a divine will. He is unlike us in that way, but we are mistaken if we think such holiness is beyond us. In fact, it was precisely the reason he became incarnate. The death and resurrection of Christ is him "instituting afresh" the human nature, as Maximus puts it.[5] It accomplishes what he calls in *Difficulty 10* "the death of death."[6] Maximus captures this thought beautifully:

> Because of this, the Creator of nature himself—who has ever heard of anything so truly awesome!—has clothed himself with our nature, without change uniting it hypostatically to himself, in order to check what has been borne away, and gather it to himself, so that, gathered to himself, our nature may no longer have any difference from him in its inclination.[7]

"No longer have any difference from him in its inclination." How. Freakin'. Awesome. This is our destiny. When Saint John writes in 1 John 3:2, "When he is revealed, we will be like him, for we will see him as he is," this is part of what he means. The best part—and the part that leaves us without excuse—is that this is

---

4. Louth, *Maximus the Confessor*, 186 (from *Opuscule* 7:80D).
5. Louth, *Maximus the Confessor*, 173, 215 (from *Difficulty* 5:1049B).
6. Louth, *Maximus the Confessor*, 127 (from *Difficulty* 10:1157C).
7. Louth, *Maximus the Confessor*, 91 (from *Letter 2: On Love* 404B–C).

possible now. We do not have to wait until heaven, and in fact we cannot wait until heaven if we want to be the kind of people for whom heaven will be a blessing.

The Father and Son sent their Spirit to indwell us precisely to make this possible. This is why Paul writes in Gal 5,

> Live by the Spirit, I say, and do not gratify the desires of the flesh. For what the flesh desires is opposed to the Spirit, and what the Spirit desires is opposed to the flesh; for these are opposed to each other, to prevent you from doing what you want. But if you are led by the Spirit, you are not subject to the law. Now the works of the flesh are obvious: fornication, impurity, licentiousness, idolatry, sorcery, enmities, strife, jealousy, anger, quarrels, dissensions, factions, envy, drunkenness, carousing, and things like these. I am warning you, as I warned you before: those who do such things will not inherit the kingdom of God.
>
> By contrast, the fruit of the Spirit is love, joy, peace, patience, kindness, generosity, faithfulness, gentleness, and self-control. There is no law against such things. And those who belong to Christ Jesus have crucified the flesh with its passions and desires. If we live by the Spirit, let us also be guided by the Spirit. Let us not become conceited, competing against one another, envying one another. (Gal 5:16–26)

The indwelling of the Spirit provides, to the individual believer, the ability, the drive, the motor, and the vision to live differently in the world. It makes it possible for us to be holy, even as our Father is holy (1 Pet 1:16). Nevertheless, our wills must be engaged. We must refuse to gratify the flesh, we must crucify the flesh, we must agree to follow the guidance of the Holy Spirit.

Many of us have tried hard to resist sin. But the call of the Spirit requires a different approach. We do not "walk in the light" (1 John 1:7) by trying not to walk in darkness. We avoid walking in darkness by trying to walk in the light, by becoming increasingly familiar with what the love of God for us and for others looks like and seeking to live out that love. We do that, and the remnants of the flesh will steadily die.

PART II | FLESH TO SPIRIT

OPPORTUNITIES TO PRACTICE

1. Find a place of solitude and silence in which you can be alone for as long as needed. Invite God to show you your sins—things you have done or thought that you ought not to have, or things you have not done or thought that you ought to have. Write them down as they come up and hold nothing back. No need to probe or try to dig things up; trust God to show you what you need to see. If tears come, let them come for as long as needed. Then—and this will be the hardest part for many—schedule a time to confess them to a friend, a spiritual mother or father, or a member of the clergy. Choose someone mature and stress to them that you will be sharing things that are painful and confidential. As you confess, offer your list up with no defense or explanation; leave off the names of others as much as possible to protect them. Once your confession is over, your friend should say simply, "The Lord has put away your sins," with your reply being simply, "Thanks be to God." Burn or otherwise destroy your list.

2. Identify one thing that you do not have and/or cannot do for yourself that causes you some level of shame. It could be the time, money, or skill to accomplish something. It might be something everyone thinks you have or are good at that you really aren't. Ask for someone to help you with that thing, but do not apologize for having to ask. Express thanks for it, but do not go overboard thanking the person out of your feelings of guilt or shame in having to ask. Vulnerability builds community.

3. Write down needs you or others have that God has not called you to act on. Commit yourself to praying about these needs but not taking any action beyond prayer. Make note of what happens in these cases. There are some times where Christians rest content with prayer only when they should be doing more to meet the need. James 2 calls out the folly of this. But there are also times where Christians falsely believe prayer is

RE-FORMED BY THE SPIRIT (INDWELLING)

just an acknowledgment of our inability to do anything helpful instead of an authoritative petition for God to act. That's what this exercise is intended to counteract.

PART III

Devil to Father

Chapter Seven

Who Is the Devil?

THERE ARE DEPTHS OF EVIL we see in the world which are unexplainable in purely human terms. Humans who torture and murder one another not for the sake of any discernible benefit but just because it occurs to them to do so—rape of infants, finding pleasure purely in the dominance of powerlessness and the ruin of innocence. There are countless other examples, but I do not wish to go on. Even the most jaded, misanthropic naturalists among us struggle to explain how humanity is capable of such horrors on its own. As Christians though, we do not have to try to explain things in this way since we believe evil has an origin beyond just human misuse of free will.

It is worth acknowledging that there are some who believe in God but find the idea of angels and demons . . . silly. Just *why* they think this is silly most cannot say. I remember giving a teaching at a parachurch group at a state university and having an audience member question with incredulity my belief in angels and demons. For someone who is committed to the truths of the Christian faith regarding the Trinity and the incarnation, the existence of a realm beyond what we can see and touch has already been granted. There seems no good reason at that point to deny the existence of beings that inhabit such a realm. And given that the teaching and ministry of Jesus are firmly committed to the reality of these beings and to the deliverance of people from the influence of demons, there is ample reason to affirm their existence.

Isaiah 14:12–15 has been interpreted in much of Christian tradition allegorically. Literally it is a rebuke of the human ruler of Babylon, but it has also been understood in both the New Testament and the early church as an origin story for supernatural evil. Isaiah writes,

> How you are fallen from heaven,
> O Day Star, son of Dawn!
> How you are cut down to the ground,
> you who laid the nations low!
> You said in your heart,
> "I will ascend to heaven;
> I will raise my throne
> above the stars of God;
> I will sit on the mount of assembly
> on the heights of Zaphon;
> I will ascend to the tops of the clouds,
> I will make myself like the Most High."
> But you are brought down to Sheol,
> to the depths of the Pit.

"Morning Star" here is translated in many older English translations, including the King James, as a proper name: Lucifer. Viewed as the most powerful of the angels, the pinnacle of the heavenly host, Lucifer was not content to serve, but wished to call the shots and be served—and as such was "brought down." In Luke 10, Jesus recounts seeing Satan ("Accuser") fall from heaven "like a flash of lightning" (Luke 10:18). Revelation 9 contains yet another prophetic account of this event: "A star that had fallen from heaven to earth" (Rev 9:1).

> The Light-Bringer became all shadow.
> The Morning Star went dim.
> Lucifer, son of Dawn, became Satan, father of darkness.

And not content to rebel alone, Rev 12:4 records that a third of the stars (interpreted as angels) were swept down by him as well.

These become the demons that harass humans and that Luke 10 records as fleeing from the name of Jesus. More on that in chapter 9.

Ezekiel 28 proceeds similarly to Isa 14, offering a rebuke of the human King of Tyre but using language that makes it quite clear something cosmic is in view as well. Though speaking allegorically of the same event as Isaiah, it does so in different language that helps us understand more. The "signet of perfection, full of wisdom and perfect in beauty" (Ezek 28:12), who was in Eden and walked the paths of God as a blameless cherub/angel, had such knowledge that "no secret [was] hidden from [it]" (Ezek 28:3). However, in verses 16-18 God pronounces his judgment and the reason for it, once again reiterating the casting down of this being:

> In the abundance of your trade
> you were filled with violence, and you sinned;
> so I cast you as a profane thing from the mountain of God,
> and the guardian cherub drove you out
> from among the stones of fire.
> Your heart was proud because of your beauty;
> *you corrupted your wisdom for the sake of your splendor.*
> I cast you to the ground;
> I exposed you before kings,
> to feast their eyes on you.
> By the multitude of your iniquities,
> in the unrighteousness of your trade,
> you profaned your sanctuaries.
> *So I brought out fire from within you;*
> *it consumed you,*
> and I turned you to ashes on the earth
> in the sight of all who saw you.
> (Ezek 28:16-18; emphasis mine)

The Scriptures heap epithet on epithet describing this evil one:

- Accuser/Adversary (Job 1-2, Zech 3, 1 Chr 21), focusing on his actions to oppose the growth and flourishing of humanity, filling our minds with shame and the sense our sins can never fully be addressed

PART III | DEVIL TO FATHER

- Serpent/Tempter (Gen 3;, Rev 12, Matt 4), focusing on his actions to draw humanity away from God and toward any number of false idols or empty substitutes
- Murderer and father of lies (John 8), focusing on his actions that lead to the destruction of human persons, including his work to suppress and distort the truth
- Leader of demons (Matt 12), focusing on his role as the architect and origin of all supernatural evil
- Lord of dung (Matt 12), emphasizing that the only kingdom he in fact rules is one of filth
- Ruler of this world (John 14) and god of this age (2 Cor 4), focusing on the power and influence he currently exerts over cultures and institutions

He is this one who is most commonly referred to as the devil or Satan (Accuser). He is the origin of all sin and evil in the world. He is the origin of rebellion against God and of all those who rebel against God. Having amassed an army of fallen angels through temptation and lies, he sought to do the same with humanity, as is recorded in Gen 3. Having become enamored with his own knowledge and thinking himself equivalent to God, he tempts Eve and Adam to do the same and succeeds—with catastrophic consequences. He tempts them in a threefold way as we see in Gen 3:6: through sustenance for the body ("good for food"), pleasure for the senses ("delight to the eyes"), and pride in oneself ("make one wise"). And they give in, joining him in the pollution he brought upon himself and the angels by bringing that pollution into themselves and the rest of creation.

And let's be clear: this is no "devil made me do it" moment. The temptation came from outside of humanity, but humanity listened, agreed, and acted. Adam would blame Eve, and Eve the serpent (Gen 3:12–13), yet no one's hand was forced. They chose, just as we now sometimes choose, to give into temptation. We too sometimes listen, agree, and act. But there was one who resisted.

Satan tries this same threefold temptation trick with Jesus in the wilderness in Matt 4: through sustenance for the body ("stones to become loaves of bread" in Matt 4:3), pleasure for the senses ("the kingdoms of the world and their splendor" in Matt 4:8), and pride in oneself (putting the Lord to the test in Matt 4:7). But Jesus doesn't fall for it, exposing the impotence of the devil so completely he has to flee.

And this is the thing to remember: in the end, the devil is a failure. A colossal failure. Despite the ravages he and his army have inflicted, are inflicting, and will (for a time) still inflict, he has lost and will lose. They are running scared (Jas 2:19, Luke 8). Yet for now, he poses a real and present danger that must be addressed if we are to thrive.

The devil has tremendous amounts of knowledge about God and about creation. With his angelic intellect, he sees and knows more about the Father than any of us, at least this side of heaven. Job makes it clear he has at least some access to the heavenly courts and that he prowls creation (Job 1:6–7). He is not omniscient (knowing everything) or omnipresent (being everywhere); only God is those. But given that angelic faculties outstrip our own human faculties, we are rightly staggered by the power and knowledge of both angels and demons. However, there is one critical kind of knowledge available to humanity that is not available to any demon, Satan included.

Demons cannot know God as Father. They can no longer be the recipients of Abba's love, mercy, and kindness. I do not say that God no longer loves them, because if God is love he cannot cease to lavish fatherly affection even on such creatures as demons. But they are unable to see, receive, know, or understand it. Having rejected God from a position of perfect knowledge and unfettered access to him, their fall was unlike that of humans, who knew and interacted with God only in part. "To whom much has been given, much will be required" (Luke 12:48). Having fallen from the highest of heights, they have now crashed down to the deepest of depths, deeper than that to which any human could descend. Having rejected the love of God despite having known it perfectly, there is now nothing to deliver them from existing as orphans. Orphans of their own choosing despite the ever-present love of God always being immeasurably close to them. As I type this I feel a gut wrenching pity for them, the kind of pity that comes from watching someone self-destruct right in front of you despite being surrounded by people who care for them and offer help. And as I type this I find myself hoping I'm wrong, hoping that God has a way to bring them back.

This "orphanhood" is really the only thing the devil has to offer. He will promise much more of course, just as the world and the flesh promise much more. But remember: he is a liar and the father of lies. Getting you to believe things that aren't true is his primary weapon. The natural pull of the world and flesh will be supernaturally intensified by the devil until they seem nearly impossible to resist. But he has no power or authority to deliver on any promise other than attempting to sever you from the love, mercy, and care of God. He will do so through a variety of means, but it almost always comes back to the same script:

"God doesn't really love you. God won't really take care of you. God doesn't really have your best interests at heart. You and your problems are too small to garner even a fraction of his attention."

"You are better off without him. You know what needs to be done. You have the power to pull it off."

Or . . .

"You are not enough and will never be enough regardless of what he does. You are too broken to save. You will never be good."

And so we see the devil for who and what he is: the source and director of the world and the flesh.

OPPORTUNITIES TO PRACTICE

1. C. S. Lewis (1898–1963) writes in *The Screwtape Letters*, "There are two equal and opposite errors into which our race can fall about the devils. One is to disbelieve in their existence. The other is to believe, and to feel an excessive and unhealthy interest in them."[1] Discuss with your group your experiences of supernatural evil, confessing any doubts you may have about the existence of demons, and repenting of any places where you feel you have given into an unhealthy interest or involvement with them.

2. Grab something to take notes on and head to a quiet place. Begin by asking God to show you any lies you have believed about yourself, about him, or about others. Write down everything he shows you. After that, go through the list one by one and ask God to show you the truth that counteracts that lie. Write down everything he shows you. Choose an example to share with your group.

3. A powerful practice with ancient roots is the renunciation of our ties with the world, the flesh, and the devil as part of our admission into the fellowship of Christ via baptism. Whether one was baptized as an infant or as a believer, it is beneficial to periodically reaffirm this commitment; many traditions do this annually on Holy Saturday.[2] Do this now with your group, choosing a leader as you see fit. Here is an example liturgy from the ACNA's 2019 Book of Common Prayer to guide you:

> *Leader:* Do you renounce the devil and all the spiritual forces of wickedness that rebel against God?

---

1. Lewis, *Screwtape Letters*, ix.
2. The Great Vigil of Holy Saturday is observed in many liturgical traditions after sunset on the day after Good Friday and before sunrise on Easter. It both commemorates Jesus's descent to Hades and anticipates his coming resurrection.

PART III | DEVIL TO FATHER

People: I renounce them.

Leader: Do you renounce the empty promises and deadly deceits of this world that corrupt and destroy the creatures of God?

People: I renounce them.

Leader: Do you renounce the sinful desires of the flesh that draw you from the love of God?

People: I renounce them.[3]

---

3. Anglican Church in North America, Book of Common Prayer, 177.

Chapter Eight

Who Is the Father?

THE FATHER IS THE First Person of the Trinity, and the source of being of the other members of the Trinity. However, we have to say a bit about this since some have falsely concluded that this means the Father is superior to the Son and the Spirit, which is absolutely not the case. Christians believe in a single God who is eternal (no beginning and no end), omnipotent (all-powerful), omniscient (all-knowing), omnibenevolent (perfectly good), and omnipresent (existing everywhere). This one God exists in three persons—Father, Son, and Holy Spirit—all of whom have always existed together and who equally share the nature, majesty, and glory of God. The church has rejected beliefs that the Son or the Spirit were inferior to the Father in any way.[1]

Because humans like to think in images, we naturally try to picture this three-in-oneness in a variety of ways. Of course every image falls short in some way both because God is not spatial and because there is nothing that exists that can perfectly represent God other than God himself. Nevertheless, pictures can be a helpful way to illustrate what might otherwise seem like abstract thoughts. Some envision a line flowing from Father to Son to Spirit; others imagine a pyramid with three sections. These have

---

1. The First Council of Nicaea (325) and the First Council of Constantinople (381) are key here.

their strengths, but one of the notable weaknesses is they suggest a hierarchy: someone has to be at the top. My preferred mental image is of a circle or sphere composed of three interlocking pieces. This has the advantage of showing how the three together form one whole and support one another without suggesting any kind of superiority or inferiority.

So if there is no inferiority within God, what is this business of the Father being the source of the Son and the Spirit, sometimes called the *monarchia* (Greek: "one rule") of the Father? Bertrand de Margerie summarizes it this way:

> The Father is the foundation and principle of intra-divine unity. It is the Father, and not the divine essence considered abstractly, who is the principle of the Son and of the Spirit; and a principle without principle, for the Father himself does not spring from some mysterious impersonal essence.[2]

Part of what this means is that God is personal (really tri-personal) to the very core. There is no divine nature prior to, undergirding, or producing the Father, Son, and Holy Spirit. If there were, we would either have to view the divine nature as the first member of a Quarternity or we would have three gods who each separately possess that divine nature (tritheism). Instead, the divine nature is the Godhead itself: it is all of the omnis listed above (and more!) as they are lived out together in the life of the Father, the Son, and the Holy Spirit. The Father is the one who is unoriginated but serves as the origin of the other two. If we want to think rightly of God as Christians, we don't start by describing an abstract divine nature and working our way to three persons. We start with the three persons and describe what makes them who they are.

When we use the word *person* here, we do not mean person in the usual sense of the word. We do not mean that in God are three distinct centers of consciousness, aware of different things and thinking different thoughts. That would again land us in

---

2. Toon, *Our Triune God*, 149.

tritheism. The Greek word that ends up getting translated into Latin as *persona* is *hypostasis*. There's not a direct English equivalent here for this Greek philosophical term, but *hypostasis* may be roughly described as an "underling principle" or "foundational reality." The idea is that the "threeness" of God goes all the way down; it is a real and true description of who God is. And yet this threeness—these three hypostases—share the same divine nature or *ousia* (Greek: "essence").

We have been highlighting what all three persons share, but what makes them different from one another? As the church has studied the Scriptures over centuries, it has rejected what is called modalism, the idea that God is really a single person who sometimes appears as Father, sometimes as Son, and sometimes as Holy Spirit.[3] That is, the Father, the Son, and the Spirit are not just "hats" God puts on and takes off, nor are they just roles all played by one person the way that I am a husband, a son, and a dad. The church has found such a view lacking because it fails to do justice to the biblical witness regarding the three persons, which describes the persons existing together and interacting with one another. To give a small sample: we see the Father sending the Son, we see the Son asking the Father to be spared from crucifixion, we see the Spirit descending upon the Son and the voice of the Father calling out from heaven, and the Son now sits at the right hand of the Father in heaven and sent the Spirit to guide the church. All of these are deceptive at best and impossible at worst if, in fact, God is not three distinct persons.

But if they are all equally God and there is only one God, what makes the persons different from one another? The thing that differentiates the persons are the ways in which they are eternally related to one another. So the Father is the one who is without origin or foundation, serving as the foundation of both the Son and the Spirit. He is the only one who can rightly be described as ungenerated, though he has never existed without the Son and the Spirit. Being the source of the Son and the Spirit does not make

---

3. The First Councils or Nicaea and Constantinople are again critical here, though theological rejection of modalism was clear even before the councils.

him better than them, just as my sons are not less than me. The Father eternally begets the Son and, together with the Son, eternally spirates (breathes out) the Spirit. This is why we describe the Father as first, the Son as second, and the Spirit as third, because of the logical order of their relationships to one another. But again and as already discussed, there is no suggestion of inferiority. There's no gold-, silver-, and bronze-medal winners. And there is no "before and after." The Father never existed without the Son and the Spirit.

If you struggle to understand this, you aren't alone. All of the examples we can see in our lives of one thing generating or producing another means the thing doing the producing had to come first. Time infects, as it were, all of our natural ways of thinking. We may not be able to do better than Gregory of Nazianzus, fourth-century Greek theologian to whom we owe much of the best of Trinitarian theology, who writes,

> Therefore, when did these [the Son and the Spirit] come into existence? They are beyond "when." But if it is necessary to say something even vigorously—when the Father did. And when did the Father come into existence? There was not [a time] when he was not. And this is the case with the Son and the Holy Spirit. Ask me again, and again I will answer you. When was the Son begotten? When the Father was not begotten. When did the Spirit proceed? When the Son was not proceeding but was timelessly begotten and beyond reason.[4]

Having laid out a bit about the eternal nature of the Father, let's move to what he Has done "for us and for our salvation," as the Nicene Creed puts it. And here I want to denounce the very common but dangerous belief that Jesus died on the cross so God would love us. Here's the truth:

The Father did not need Jesus to die in order to love you.

I want you to slow down and read that again: the Father did not need Jesus to die in order to love you.

---

4. Rusch, *Trinitarian Controversy*, 106 (from Gregory of Nazianzus's *Third Theological Oration* §3).

WHO IS THE FATHER?

If we think that the effects of sin are so drastic that the Father cannot love us without a sacrifice, we have fundamentally misunderstood the love of God and vastly overestimated the power of sin. The Father sends the Son to save us *because* he loves us, not *so that* he can love us. The Father's love—the love of the Trinity—is what ensures sin is not the end of the story. Salvation isn't the restoration of God's love for humanity; it is the overcoming of everything that would keep humanity from receiving that love.

> So if anyone is in Christ, there is a new creation: everything old has passed away; see, everything has become new! All this is from God, who reconciled us to himself through Christ, and has given us the ministry of reconciliation; that is, in Christ God was reconciling the world to himself, not counting their trespasses against them, and entrusting the message of reconciliation to us. (2 Cor 5:17–19)

Word order matters here: it is not God who needed to be reconciled to us, but us to God. Jesus's sacrifice doesn't increase God's love for us; it allows and empowers us to love God. It changes *us* to restore the union and communion which were lost by our sin. It addresses our sins and trespasses so that we are not only reconciled to him—brought home to depth of intimate relationship—but so that we are fit to be carriers of that same reconciliation to others.

Make no mistake: there is a reason why you struggle to view the love of the Father this way, and it isn't simply that you are dense or closed down. The effect of imbibing the message of the devil is to conclude that, because of our sin, the Father must hate us and that we have to hide to avoid being exposed. Remember what Adam and Eve did immediately after committing the first sin? They hid their bodies with fig leaf bikinis in Gen 3:7 (a poor substitute for the actual protection God would later provide them in animal skins in Gen 3:21). And when he came close and called to them, they hid themselves further (Gen 3:8). They felt shame, they felt fear, and so they hid.

We have mistaken shame for repentance. We have confused feeling really bad about ourselves with turning toward God. We have mistaken self-flagellation for seeking restoration with God through acknowledgment of wrong-doing. This is the illusion of holiness; this is having a form of a thing but denying its power. This is the flesh. Shame kills. This is why Judas hangs himself after betraying Jesus (Matt 27:5). Repentance produces life. This is why Peter ends up fit to strengthen his brothers and lead the fledgling church (John 21:15–17). Yet the habit of thinking the Father is just waiting to bust us runs deep. Why?

We learn models of parenthood and authority from our lived experiences, and none of us has had a perfect human parent or authority figure. Some of us have had radically imperfect ones, with relationships full of guilt, shame, manipulation, outright deception, abuse, or abandonment. Many of us have suffered from unrealistic expectations, emotional unavailability, passivity that leads to harm, or have been denied physical and verbal affection. All of us have been misunderstood, gone unheard, been treated unfairly. The more common and extreme these experiences, and the earlier in childhood they happen, the more dramatic the effect they have on us and our views of the Father—and the more we have to unlearn.

The only posture with which one can come to the Father and benefit is one of vulnerability. But many of us have seen that vulnerability with parents or authority figures can produce suffering, or at least not lead to anything helpful. So we've adopted habits of thinking and feeling designed to protect ourselves. Some seem quite holy on the surface but serve to reinforce the idea that the Father is aloof and unavailable, like stressing his transcendence over all creation but failing to emphasize his routine and active involvement in it. Some seem neutral but are designed to protect ourselves from disappointment, like staying so busy that we fail to make time for basic disciplines like prayer and biblical study. And some we know are wrong but do them anyway, like staying away from Christian community when we are struggling with sin until we know we're "on a good stretch" and can come back. In summary, we are able to identify in ourselves the tendency to act and think like orphans, to live as if we have no parent who cares for us and so have to do things on our own. As we have already discussed at length the three causes of this way of operating, how do we go about correcting these mistaken ways of viewing the Father?

One important move to make in our thoughts is to change our concept of what it means to be a father. Ephesians 3:14–15 says, "For this reason I bow my knees before the Father, from whom every family [or *fatherhood*] in heaven and on earth takes its name." Despite the ease and naturalness of the move, it is not our experience of parenthood that gets to define what it means for God to be Father. It is instead God who gets to define what parenthood is and means, and the rest of us as parents are to commit ourselves to parenting that way. Now this requires repeated, intentional retraining of our minds because our experiences powerfully and importantly inform our thoughts, and we don't change these concepts by just trying to think differently. However, we do have to try to think differently. Studying the biblical notion of parenthood, as rooted in the revealed character of the Father, is an important part of the conversion of our thinking.

When we are struggling to relate properly to God as Father, it can be helpful to remind ourselves that it is Jesus's relationship to God as Father that best reveals the heart of the Father. The Father cherishes Jesus, honors him, and lifts him up. The Father is quick to respond to Jesus, meeting every need. And because we have been united with Christ by faith, we can be assured the Father relates similarly to us.

It is also helpful to remember that the love of Jesus *just is* the love of the Father. They are not separate loves. The thoughts of Jesus for us are the thoughts of the Father, the thoughts of the Trinity. There is only one divine mind and divine will, and they are shared equally and completely by Father, Son, and Holy Spirit. What Jesus thinks of you, the Father and Spirit think of you. What Jesus wants for you, the Father and Spirit want for you. And they always act together to bring it to pass!

PART III | DEVIL TO FATHER

OPPORTUNITIES TO PRACTICE

1. Listen to the song "Good Good Father" by Chris Tomlin.[5] Now listen to it again. What thoughts or emotions come up? Which parts resonate with you? Which parts do you struggle with?

2. For most of us, our views of the Father have been shaped—for good and for ill—by our experiences of our parents and other authority figures. Find a place of solitude and silence where you can reflect for a while. Start by asking God to show you the ways authority figures have hurt or angered you. As things come up, forgive them by praying something like this: "In Jesus's name I choose to forgive [name] for [thing they did]. I ask that you not hold their sins against them, and I choose to bless them."

3. Discuss with your group places where you are afraid of asking the Father to work more strongly with you. Bring up the fears and vulnerabilities you have, what you worry will happen or could happen if you invite the Father to "o'erthrow" you. What are the roots of these fears? What is the cost of not inviting the Father to do what needs to be done?

4. Make a list of all the things that come to your mind when you think of fatherhood. Don't edit the list or hold anything back. Once complete, put a check mark by everything on the list that you think accurately describes the Father. Put an X by everything on the list that does not describe him. For the X's, reflect on where those associations came from for you.

5. Find an older, spiritually mature Christian that you know and trust. This could be one of your parents, someone from your church, or someone you know in a different context, but it should be someone who knows you well and has poured into your life. Ask them to pray that you would better know and receive the love of the Father. If you are comfortable and think they would be as well, ask them to pray a blessing over you.

5. Tomlin, "Good Good Father."

Chapter Nine

Re-Formed by the Father (Imitation)

I WANT TO BRING us back to the sonnet by Donne cited in the introduction and highlight the difference in God's action. He notes that God has acted in the following ways, but mourns that they have not been enough to set him free:

Knock
Breathe
Shine
Seek to mend

Each of these verbs highlight the gentleness with which the Father has dealt with Donne. I think back to Matt 12:20: "He will not break a bruised reed." The Father has been present and active, but in ways that are inviting rather than demanding, accommodating rather than disruptive. Yet Donne finds himself unable to "rise and stand," and so invites the Father to "o'erthrow [him]":

Break
Blow
Burn
Make me new

PART III | DEVIL TO FATHER

I love how each of these verbs is an intensification of a verb from the prior set. The Father maintains the same ways of acting, but dials up the heat. I think here of Heb 12:26–29:

> At that time [when God revealed the Law to Israel on Mount Sinai] his voice shook the earth; but now he has promised, "Yet once more I will shake not only the earth but also the heaven." This phrase, "Yet once more," indicates the removal of what is shaken—that is, created things—so that what cannot be shaken may remain. Therefore, since we are receiving a kingdom that cannot be shaken, let us give thanks, by which we may offer to God an acceptable worship with reverence and awe; for indeed our God is a consuming fire.

Everything that can be shaken will be shaken and removed so that only those things which cannot be shaken will remain. The only things that ultimately will be able to "rise and stand" will be the things that cannot be shaken, so we need everything else cleared. This is another place in which the foundry makes an appearance since "our God is a consuming fire."

So if this kind of action is what is needed, why does the Father waste time with the gentle stuff? First, the gentle workings are what create the hunger and thirst needed to make the prayer. Remember, in the same way that human will was complicit in the fall of humanity and is complicit in the sins we commit now, it must also be complicit in redemption. It is very often through the gentle workings of the Father that we see ourselves as we are and find the desire to change. Second, the gentle workings are what build trust in the nature and character of the Father. Most of us are so enthralled with our own self-determination and self-rule that the idea of inviting the Father to upend that is a nonstarter. We are terrified of the loss of predictability, the loss of familiarity, and the loss of control. And if we are going to get to the point where we beg the Father to snatch those idols from us, we are going to have to be very, very convinced he knows what he's doing and wants what is good for us.

The great truth of the foundry is revealed by Isa 33:14–16:

RE-FORMED BY THE FATHER (IMITATION)

> The sinners in Zion are afraid; trembling has seized the
>   godless:
> "Who among us can live with the devouring fire?
> Who among us can live with everlasting flames?"
> Those who walk righteously and speak uprightly,
> who despise the gain of oppression,
> who wave away a bribe instead of accepting it,
> who stop their ears from hearing of bloodshed
> and shut their eyes from looking on evil,
> they will live on the heights;
> their refuge will be the fortresses of rocks;
> their food will be supplied, their water assured.

There is no escaping everlasting flames. To dwell with God—to live on the heights—is to be surrounded by fire, engulfed by flame. The difference for "those who walk righteously and speak uprightly" is the effect the fire has: it ceases to be a devouring fire and becomes a fire of provision. It isn't the fire that changes but us. As we drink deeply of the love of the triune God and practice imitating his way of being in the world, we are transformed. We become like the burning bush in Exod 3 and 4, on fire with the presence of God, a vehicle for that presence which is not damaged in the least.

In a foundry, when the metal has been suitably purified and any needed chemicals have been added, the metal is then poured into molds to be given the desired shape. The material the patterns/molds are made of has to melt at a higher temperature than what is being melted. Otherwise the pattern will be destroyed and the precious metal lost. When the Scriptures talk about God as a devouring fire, it is not that God gets joy out of destruction. It is that inferior molds—not just sinful molds, but even merely human molds—simply are not up to the job. They are not the kind of patterns that can fit us for heaven.

Because the patterns of the world are broken and deficient in the same way our humanity is since the fall, when we conform to them we suffer, we fail, we despair. We think we're the problem, but we've just chosen the wrong pattern. "The mass of [people] live lives of quiet desperation," Henry David Thoreau famously writes in *Walden*.[1] Yet most of us feel incredible pressure to match those around us, to not rock the boat. God's call to us in Rom 12 is to "present [our] bodies as a living sacrifice" and to "not be conformed to this world, but be transformed by the renewing of [our] minds" (Rom 12:1–2). So, what are we supposed to conform to if not the pattern that is all around us?

The pattern for all of us is the image of the triune God as revealed most clearly in Jesus. That is, the same pattern in which we have been created/made is the pattern into which we are being re-created/re-made. When the Scriptures speak of God as both Alpha and Omega, beginning and end, this is part of what is meant. God is our beginning in the sense that he is our Creator and the one in whose image or mold we were created. That image was broken and weakened in the fall, but not destroyed. We are being remade into the same mold in which we were originally cast; we are being melted down and purified so that our former glory can be restored and even expanded. Our "middle" may be messy, but our beginning and our end are most assuredly not!

However, nothing finite can fully reflect the infinite. So though we will all be in the pattern of the Trinity, we will all look different. The expectation isn't pale, dull conformance to some merely human standard or mold. As we conform to the pattern of God, to the pattern God has specifically for us, we will keep certain distinctions. We will not just still be ourselves, we will be more ourselves than we have ever been. And this begins now.

Imitation is the way we begin inhabiting this pattern, living into it here and now. Paul says in 1 Cor 11:1, "Be imitators of me, as I am of Christ." The overwhelming majority of Christians, including Paul, never got to lay eyes on Christ in the flesh. Therefore to learn this way of living, we study the Scriptures and we watch how holy people in our own lifetimes model Christ. Imitation of Christ, who himself imitates the Father, is commanded here and now as a means of our transformation. As Jas 1:21 puts it, "Therefore rid yourselves of all sordidness and rank growth of wickedness, and

---

1. Thoreau, *Walden*, 7.

RE-FORMED BY THE FATHER (IMITATION)

welcome with meekness the implanted word that has the power to save your souls." But what does that mean and how do we do it?

Before we undertake the grace-filled work of seeking to be more like Jesus, it is important to deal with the spiritual blockages that will make the work harder and less fruitful. Demonic opposition can make the grace of God harder to sense, which in turn makes the work of spiritual discipline and discipleship feel nearly insurmountable. To be clear, learning to deal with spiritual opposition is something that occurs repeatedly as we mature through the course of our lives; it is not merely something to do at the outset of the journey. But we are wise to learn and practice these things early as they will make the path of spiritual growth easier to walk.

We cannot take the life and ministry of Jesus as indicative of how we are to live without quickly coming to the conclusion that demons are real and active, and that those who are in Christ are equipped and commanded to deal with them (Mark 16:17). We cannot believe demons are just a naïve, premodern way of explaining physical or mental illness without also believing we are smarter than the Incarnate God. Instead, if we wish to partner with Christ and become increasingly like him, we must join him in the work of resisting the devil in our own lives and in delivering others from the influence of such powers. While there is nothing like a single model of deliverance from the demonic in the Scriptures, there are numerous passages that provide examples and illustrate critical principles:

- Deliverance will always be in the name of Jesus, not in our own name and authority (Luke 10). It is from Jesus that we receive this authority, it is at Jesus's command that we are sent out to exercise it, and it is through focusing our lives on him (living in his name) and through verbal use of his name ("In Jesus's name, I command you to leave") that we will be effective.

- Jesus has already defeated the powers of hell (Heb 2:14–15, Col 2:15). Helping people get free is not the waging of a new war, the outcome of which is uncertain. It is taking the message of a victory already won and proclaiming it into a particular situation.

- Practices that deepen our relationship with and trust in Jesus increase the authority which we carry (Matt 17:14-20, Mark 9:14-29). Note that in these cases, Jesus's message to his disciples wasn't that the demons were so strong that he could do it and they couldn't. Instead there was an increase of faith needed, an increase which is supported by practices such as prayer and fasting (though the latter does not appear in the most reliable manuscripts of these verses).

- Deliverance isn't an end unto itself but a means to an end (Matt 12:43-45). We are freed from the power and influence of the demonic so that we are free to embrace God and to reorder our lives increasingly around him. To be set free but not to make such changes can worsen things for us; "to whom much is given, much is expected" (Luke 12:48). If we help others get free, we need to kindly and without fear remind them of this fact.

- We need not allow demons to speak or to make a show (Matt 12:29, Luke 4:35). Jesus routinely forbids demons to speak when they were going to reveal his identity before the appointed time. Similarly, we may command demons to be silent in Jesus's name to prevent spreading lies or inducing fear.

There is much more that could be said as there are numerous books written on exercising authority over the demonic, and some traditions even have training programs on the subject. The majority of such encounters are short and relatively peaceful compared to the Hollywood portrayals of exorcism. There's no need of shouting or threatening the demons as they, quite frankly, aren't scared of you but of Jesus. Make sure the person with such an affliction feels loved and safe, exercise the authority you've been given, and focus on deepening your own love of God and growth into Christlikeness. Do these and you'll be well-equipped to help others.

And what about this growth into Christlikeness, the increase in personal holiness and decrease of fleshly ways of thinking and

RE-FORMED BY THE FATHER (IMITATION)

behaving? When Jesus says at the end of Matt 5, "Be perfect, therefore, as your heavenly Father is perfect" (Matt 5:48), he is capping off a stunning teaching in which he has eviscerated any notion of moderate religion or measured devotion. Don't just keep your hands from murder; keep your heart away from anger that leads you to demean others. Don't just avoid cheating on your spouse; be ruthless in conquering your lust. Don't just make sure to satisfy the legal demands of divorce; acknowledge that anything that would justify a divorce is already a deeply problematic and sinful state of affairs. Don't just make good on your promises; be a person of your word and avoid any flourishes or exaggerated performances. Don't just avoid retribution or recompense that is over the top; give without restraint, even to those who have treated you unjustly and even when it is uncomfortable. Don't just love your neighbor; love in both word and deed the ones who hate you, committing yourself even to be fervent in prayer that the Lord would bless them. And (though this goes beyond Matt 5) do all of this without marveling that you've done it or even giving it a second thought.

As I hope you have seen from this book, this kind of holiness is possible. It takes a reception of everything on offer to us in the triune God and the willingness to grow via practice over time, but it is possible. Hebrews 12 pulls no punches about the ways in which we must imitate Christ in his sufferings; we are to "lay aside every weight and the sin that clings so closely," to "run with perseverance the race that is set before us," to "not grow weary or lose heart," and to "endure trials for the sake of discipline" (Heb 12:1–7). It is the gracious parenting of the Father on our behalf that develops us into maturity. We are bolstered by "so great a cloud of witnesses," numerous examples of faithful women and men over time who have lived this way, providing us both assurance that it is possible and examples of what to aim for.

And so we are commanded to "pursue peace with everyone, and the holiness without which no one will see the Lord. *See to it that no one fails to obtain the grace of God*; that no root of bitterness springs up and causes trouble, and through it many become defiled" (Heb 12:14–15; emphasis mine). What is striking to me here is that the phrase translated "see to it" has the same root word as bishop or overseer (Greek: *episcopos*). The idea is that we bear some responsibility for others in community and are to accept this responsibility. It isn't simply pastors and teachers who are responsible for the care of souls; it is an expectation for each member of the community. By the grace of God, I am responsible for growing in holiness, for receiving help from others in doing so, and for providing such help to others. It is not enough merely to maintain peace in the community if such peace depends on shirking our responsibility to help one another grow. Being in the foundry means becoming part of the foundry.

In addition to resistance of explicit demonic forces and the overcoming of personal sin, we must also commit to joining Jesus in meeting human needs. "Religion that is pure and undefiled before God, the Father, is this: to care for orphans and widows in their distress, and to keep oneself unstained by the world" (Jas 1:27). It is not enough to keep our hearts and lives "clean" and watch the world around us burn. It is not enough to overcome personal lust but rest content with the sex trade, to rein in personal anger but allow systemic racism to persist, to kill greed in ones' own soul but remain passive in the face economic injustice. Thus Charles Gore can write, "We deny the veracity of the Incarnation in its principle if we deny the Christian spirit the privilege, aye, and the obligation, to concern itself with everything that interests and touches human life."[2]

However, this concern for others and for society at large does not follow only from the doctrine of the incarnation but flows directly out of the orthodox doctrine of creation. I've used the following analogy in the past to describe this important truth. Suppose you and I are good friends. We hang out frequently with one another, know each other's families, and even share some common interests and hobbies. But secretly, unbeknownst to you, I play darts at night. And not with just a regular dartboard: this dartboard has a picture of you in the center. And every time the picture

---

2. Gray, *Earth and Altar*, 128.

gets too crumpled and hole-ridden to be serviceable, I replace it with a fresh picture, always of you.

What would you think and feel if you found out? Would you conclude we weren't really friends? Would you start looking back over our interactions for evidence of ill intent? Of course. And why?

Because how we treat the image of someone reflects what we think of that person.

And so if every human is created in the image of God, mistreatment of humans is in a meaningful sense mistreatment of God himself. This is why in Matt 25 Jesus can equate service "of the least of these" with service of Christ himself, and use it as a criteria by which sheep and goats will be separated from one another. This is why in the Old Testament prophets, idolatry and injustice are so closely linked. Jeremiah weaves critique of godlessness and critique of greed and oppression throughout his writings:

- Jeremiah 5 attributes both personal sin and injustice to a lack of the fear of the Lord.

- Jeremiah 7 says that the people should not content themselves with the temple but that if they wish God to dwell with them—to truly dwell with them—they must "act justly one with another," "not oppress the alien, the orphan, and the widow or shed innocent blood," and "not go after other gods to your own hurt" (Jer 7:5–6).

- Jeremiah 22 reiterates this dual focus on justice and faithfulness to God, both calling the nation to repentance and praising King Josiah: "He judged the cause of the poor and needy; then it was well. *Is not this to know me?* says the Lord" (Jer 22:16; emphasis mine).

Jeremiah is a particularly clear example of this, but you can see these same themes repeated throughout the major and minor prophets, and in the ethics of the New Testament. Tolerance of injustice is irreconcilable with the good news; it is aligned with hell rather than heaven.

PART III | DEVIL TO FATHER

We are instead called to live a life of what Letty Russell (1929–2007) in *The Future of Partnership* calls "advent shock," to live in such a way that we are "infected with hope," working to transform the present into the image of God's future.[3] Many of us live in a kind of resigned despair, feeling overwhelmed by the magnitude of needs around us and convinced of our inability to do much about it. The call here is not simply to work, because a great many work themselves into bitterness and exhaustion. Instead the call is to reflect deeply on the way in which the incarnation has forever changed human history, consider what that means about God's commitment to all of humanity, and receive from him the strength needed to fight. For Russell, this fighting is characterized by three forms of service to others: curative (healing ills), preventative (preventing social ills), and prospective (opening the horizon for human flourishing).

There is real, meaningful work to be done as the church takes stock of the ills of the present and works to address them, yet even human effort empowered by the Spirit is insufficient to bring this vision to fruition. We need the one who inaugurated the kingdom to return and fulfill it; we need the Second Coming of our Lord and our God. What we have come to in part and what we are promised we one day will come to in fullness is "Mount Zion and to the city of the living God, the heavenly Jerusalem, and to innumerable angels in festal gathering, and to the assembly of the firstborn who are enrolled in heaven, and to God the judge of all, and to the spirits of the righteous made perfect, and to Jesus, the mediator of a new covenant" (Heb 12:22–24).

And as we await the perfection to come, we are called to imitate the Father by imitating the Son by the power of the Spirit:

>to work for a world of love and justice,
>to pursue lives rife with holiness,
>to overcome the demonic.

---

3. Russell, *Future of Partnership*, 102–3.

RE-FORMED BY THE FATHER (IMITATION)

OPPORTUNITIES TO PRACTICE

1. Find a trusted friend and talk to them about your experience of your father (or mother if you haven't known your father). Share with your friend about the parts of your parent you admire and the ways in which you were loved well. Open up to them about a way in which you were hurt or wounded by your parent, a way in which a legitimate need wasn't met. The point here isn't to blame or to shame your parent but to recognize the way in which others can shape us just as we can shape others.

2. Take an area in which you struggle to trust the Father and give to someone in need generously and sacrificially. It could be finances, time, sleep, or something else entirely. Do not share with the group what you gave or to whom, but talk through what opposition you may have felt and how you handled it.

3. Discuss with your group one of the descriptions of Christlike holiness that strikes you as most difficult to live out. Brainstorm together possible ways of practicing this virtue, and commit to practicing together.

4. One of the most difficult things for many people to do is to confront someone else about something they are doing that is hurting themselves or someone else, or something that is a blind spot for that person in their own growth. I have had cases in which the Lord has brought such people and scenarios to mind and I have hesitated to act, sometimes until it was too late. If you are aware of any scenario like this, commit to praying for that person regularly and strongly consider whether meeting privately to discuss it would benefit them. My best friends are, without fail, the people who have had the courage to confront me about my mess.

Conclusion

IN THE FLIGHT AWAY from God, humanity took the initiative. Through the bare and unfounded exercise of our will, prompted as it was by the temptations of the serpent, we insisted on our own way and received it. Through the rejection of a life of ongoing dependence on the One-in-Three and Three-in-One who created us in love, we partially severed the connection between us and him, between us and others, and between us and ourselves. Note the trifold nature of our fall in the disintegration of these relationships, the effect of which was to subject ourselves and all creation to decay and death.

The fall began with the initiative of humanity but ended with the initiative of God as he pronounced the curses and consequences of what had happened, concluding with banishment from paradise (Gen 3:14–21). But even in this, God is setting the stage for redemption and extending grace, clothing them with animal skins (sacrificial skins!) to protect them and banishing them temporarily for their good. Can you imagine the misery of creatures subject to a cycle of decay and death that would never end? It is the mercy of God which makes the tree of life unavailable until the effects of the fall could be remedied.

In the flight back into God, God takes the initiative. The incarnation is the sending of the Son by the Father, which makes the indwelling possible. The indwelling is the sending of the Spirit by both Father and Son, which makes imitation possible. Imitation is the necessary individual response for the initiative of God to accomplish its purpose in the human mind and will. The human will, which was the vehicle of our damnation, becomes the vehicle of our salvation first by being assumed and perfected in Christ, second in being transformed and strengthened in individuals indwelled by the Spirit, and third by being exercised by redeemed believers within a community of redeemed believers doing the same.

Why do we embrace the Trinity as both one to be loved and a doctrine to be professed? Because, quite simply, the only God capable of saving us is just such a God. As Herman Bavinck (1854–1921) in *The Doctrine of God* writes,

> Religion cannot afford to be satisfied with anything less than God. In Christ God himself comes to us, and in the Holy Spirit he imparts himself to us. The work of redemption is thoroughly Trinitarian in character. Of God, and through God, and in God are all things.
>
> It is one divine act from beginning to end. Nevertheless it reveals a threefold distinction: it is summarised in the love of the Father, the grace of the Son, and the communion of the Holy Spirit. . . .
>
> The triune God is the source of every blessing we receive. He is the mainspring of our entire salvation. In his name we are baptised: that name is the summary of our confession; that name is the source of all blessings that descend upon us; that name is and remains eternally the object of our praise and adoration; in that name we find rest for our soul, and peace for our conscience. Above, before and within him, the Christian has a God.[1]

Though I have broken things up in terms of encountering or being shaped by the Father, Son, or Spirit separately, the truth is far better than that. We can never only encounter one member of the Trinity because God doesn't have parts. What we encounter in each of the persons is God himself: undiluted, undivided God.

As the members of the Trinity have been together for all eternity, so too they are always together now. To be shaped by the Father, for example, is to be shaped by the Son and the Spirit as well.

---

1. Bavinck, *Doctrine of God*, 333–34.

Psychologically, things can differ: we may feel an ease with the Son but be suspicious of the Spirit. But the Son never comes without the Spirit. And as we mature, God will reshape us, deepening our communion with each of the persons individually and collectively.

This encounter with the triune God is precisely the fire of the foundry! Or put differently, it is the fiery love of the threefold God playing out in history which purifies us. And since the Father, Son, and Spirit have existed together from all eternity, the fire was kindled before creation began. The fire we are to draw close to is the loving relationship between the members of the Trinity:

> I ask not only on behalf of these, but also on behalf of those who will believe in me through their word, that they may all be one. As you, Father, are in me and I am in you, may they also be in us, so that the world may believe that you have sent me. The glory that you have given me I have given them, so that they may be one, as we are one, I in them and you in me, that they may become completely one, so that the world may know that you have sent me and have loved them even as you have loved me. Father, I desire that those also, whom you have given me, may be with me where I am, to see my glory, which you have given me because you loved me before the foundation of the world. (John 17:20–24)

What God invites us into in Christ is the life of giving and receiving of the Trinity. This is why so many of the exercises in each chapter focus on either giving or receiving from one another. It is also why we have to drink deeply of the love on offer from Christ before we can have anything meaningful to give that will benefit others. "You received without payment; give without payment" (Matt 10:8). Only God is sufficient in and of himself; the rest of us have to receive. But if we never allow receipt to lead to gift, if we never engage ourselves in sacrificial service to others, we will never look like Jesus and will lack the fullness of what he came to give.

As Christians, we believe that the coming of Christ has inaugurated the kingdom of God and, thus, the eschaton (the theological name for the "end times" derived from the Greek word for "last,

CONCLUSION

furthest, uttermost"). The thing that holds together the present and the future is a life of love flowing from the Father, centered on the Son, and empowered by the Spirit. We are called to live in such a way that we are working to transform the present into the image of God's future.

But this love is no mere sentimentality. As we have seen, God's love can be like a fire, purifying us from those things which need to be removed for us to become who we are supposed to be. And it is a love that places demands on us, as we see in the prophetic vision of Ezekiel on the impending Jewish exile:

> Woe to the bloody city! I will even make the pile great. Heap up the logs, kindle the fire; boil the meat well, mix in the spices, let the bones be burned. Stand it empty upon the coals, so that it may become hot, its copper glow, its filth melt in it, its rust be consumed. In vain I have wearied myself; its thick rust does not depart. To the fire with its rust! *Yet, when I cleansed you in your filthy lewdness, you did not become clean from your filth*; you shall not again be cleansed until I have satisfied my fury upon you. (Ezek 24:9–14; emphasis mine)

This is the God of the foundry, the triune God, the one who is willing to pour out his fury (his wrath) on sin in order to separate us from it. And this isn't an isolated case. Amos 4 records the afflictions God brought upon his people: drought, blight, mildew, pestilence. "'Yet you did not return to me,' says the Lord" (Amos 4:9).

It is common (and easy!) to see wrath as antithetical to love, to dismiss the notion of divine wrath as a holdover from ancient cultures. We often think we know better now, after all. H. Richard Niebuhr (1894–1962) famously critiques this view with a simple summary of it: "A God without wrath brought men without sin into a kingdom without judgment through the ministrations of a Christ without a Cross."[2]

However, those of us who have felt the weight of sin—who have been wrecked by the world, the flesh, and the devil—have

---

2. Niebuhr, *Kingdom of God*, 193.

no such theology available to us. Many of us still struggle with the notion of God's wrath, at least partly because we have seen so few examples of healthy, godly wrath. We have seen so many examples of wrath that is unhinged, that is oriented more to making the one with wrath "feel" better instead of bringing a solution to the actual problem.

But God isn't unhinged or needy and neither is his wrath. God's wrath is precisely his love working against those things which harm those he loves. And because of this, a simple truth strikes us:

A God without wrath is a God without love.

A wrathless God can be sentimental. He can, perhaps, mean well.

But he can't be loving.

In the same way the fire had to be kindled high to melt filth and consume rust, the things which besiege us require a strong response. When we say that Christ bore the wrath of God on the cross, we do not mean that God was angry with us and instead chose to be angry with the Son. As we saw in chapter 3, such a doctrine is incoherent in light of the Trinity. What we mean is God was so attached to freeing the world of the roots and effects of sin that he did not stop short of suffering on the cross (in the person of the Son) to bring it about.

But as Ezekiel highlights, it is possible to resist the cleansing work of God on our behalf. While it is not possible for God to work and for us to miss it by some string of bad luck, it is possible to for us to reject it or to refuse it. This is why Jesus told the parable of the sower (Matt 13). This is why the writer of Hebrews warns so strongly against falling away after drinking deeply of the grace of God (Heb 6). And this is why Jesus says in Luke, "If any want to become my followers, let them deny themselves and take up their cross daily and follow me. For those who want to save their life will lose it, and those who lose their life for my sake will save it" (Luke 9:23-24). We will lose our lives, though by this he does not mean that literally everyone will be a martyr, though some will. But all of us will have to lose life as we know it—put to death our natural

CONCLUSION

ways of thinking, feeling, and behaving—in order to embrace a new way of being human. Except for more than two thousand years now, this isn't really "new."

The incarnation of Christ brought this kind of humanity into existence.

The indwelling of the Holy Spirit makes this kind of humanity a possibility for individuals and communities.

The imitation of Christ, who imitates the Father, makes this kind of humanity a reality in individuals and communities.

Bibliography

Abraham, William J. *Crossing the Threshold of Divine Revelation*. Eerdmans, 2006.
Abraham, William J., et al., eds. *Canonical Theism: A Proposal for Theology and the Church*. Eerdmans, 2008.
Anglican Church in North America. *The Book of Common Prayer*. Anglican Liturgy, 2019.
Aquinas, Thomas. *Summa Theologica*. Vol. 3. Translated by Fathers of the English Dominican Province. Christian Classics, 1948.
Augustine. *The Trinity (De Trinitate)*. 2nd ed. Translated by Edmund Hill. The Works of Saint Augustine. Edited by John E. Rotelle. New City, 2012.
Bavinck, Herman. *The Doctrine of God*. Translated by William Hendriksen. Baker, 1977.
Brown, Francis, et al. *The Brown-Driver-Briggs Hebrew and English Lexicon*. Hendrickson Academic, 2015.
Cloud, Henry, and John Townsend. *Boundaries Updated and Expanded Edition: When to Say Yes, How to Say No to Take Control of Your Life*. Zondervan, 2017.
Danker, Frederick W., et al. *Greek-English Lexicon of the New Testament and Other Early Christian Literature*. 4th ed. University of Chicago Press, 2021.
De Margerie, Bertrand. *The Christian Trinity in History*. Translated by Edmund J. Fortman. Studies in Historical Theology 1. St. Bede's, 1982.
Donne, John. "XIV. Batter My Heart, Three-Person'd God." In *The Complete Poetry and Selected Prose of John Donne*. Edited by Charles M. Coffin. Modern Library, 2001.
Emory, Gilles, and Matthew Levering, eds. *The Oxford Handbook of the Trinity*. Oxford University Press, 2014.
Foster, Richard. *Celebration of Discipline*. Anniversary ed. HarperOne, 2018.
Gray, Donald. *Earth and Altar: The Evolution of the Parish Communion in the Church of England to 1945*. Canterbury, 1986.
Herbert, George. "Love (III)." Poets.org. https://poets.org/poem/love-iii.
Lewis, C. S. *The Screwtape Letters*. HarperOne, 2001.
Louth, Andrew. *Maximus the Confessor*. Routledge, 1996.

BIBLIOGRAPHY

Luft, Joseph, and Harrington Ingham. "The Johari Window, a Graphic Model of Interpersonal Awareness." *Proceedings of the Western Training Laboratory in Group Development*. University of California, Los Angeles. Originally presented in 1955.

Marshall, Bruce. *The World, the Flesh, and Father Smith*. Houghton Mifflin, 1945.

Metz, Johannes Baptist. *Poverty of Spirit*. Translated by John Drury. Paulist, 1998.

Niebuhr, H. Richard. *The Kingdom of God in America*. Harper & Brothers, 1959.

Owen, John. *Communion with the Triune God*. Crossway, 2007.

———. *On Temptation and the Mortification of Sin in Believers*. Philadelphia, 1860. https://archive.org/details/ontemptationmortooowen/mode/2up.

Rusch, William G., ed. *The Trinitarian Controversy*. Sources of Early Christian Thought. Fortress, 1980.

Russell, Letty M. *The Future of Partnership*. Westminster, 1979.s

Schaff, Philip. *The Creeds of Christendom*. Vol. 2. New York, 1877.

Symeon the New Theologian. *The Discourses*. Translated by C. J. DeCatanzaro. Paulist, 1980.

Ten Elshof, Gregg A. *I Told Me So: Self-Deception and the Christian Life*. Eerdmans, 2009.

Tenth Avenue North. "Healing Begins." Track 1 on *The Light Meets the Dark*. Produced by Jason Ingram, Phillip LaRue, and Rusty Varenkamp. Provident Label Group, 2010.

Thoreau, Henry David. *"Walden" and Other Writings of Henry David Thoreau*. Edited by Brooks Atkinson. Random House, 1950.

Tomlin, Chris, voc. "Good Good Father." Track 1 on *Never Lose Sight*. Written by Tony Brown and Pat Barrett of Housefires. Produced by Ed Cash, Jeremy Edwardson, and Ross Copperman. Sixstepsrecords, 2016.

Toon, Peter. *Our Triune God: A Biblical Portrayal of the Trinity*. BridgePoint, 1996.

Watson, Thomas. *The Doctrine of Repentance*. Banner of Truth Trust, 1987.

Wilken, Robert Louis. *The First Thousand Years: A Global History of Christianity*. Yale University Press, 2013.

www.ingramcontent.com/pod-product-compliance
Lightning Source LLC
Chambersburg PA
CBHW070501090426
42735CB00012B/2646